PENGUIN BOOKS

EARLY DAYS

Miss Read, or in real life Mrs Dora Saint, is a teacher by profession, who started writing after the Second World War, beginning with light essays written for *Punch* and other journals. She has written on educational and country matters and worked as a script-writer for the BBC. Miss Read is married to a retired schoolmaster, and they have one daughter. They live in a tiny Berkshire hamlet. She is a local magistrate, and her hobbies are theatre-going, listening to music and reading.

Miss Read is the author of numerous books, which have gained immense popularity for their humorous and honest depictions of English rural life, including, most recently, *Farewell to Fairacre* and *The Year at Thrush Green*. Many of her books are published by Penguin, together with seven omnibus editions. She has also written several books for children, including the Red Bus series for the very young (published in one volume by Puffin as *The Little Red Bus and Other Stories*), a cookery book, *Miss Read's Country Cooking*, and two autobiographical works, *A Fortunate Grandchild* and *Time Remembered*, published together in this volume, with a new foreword by the author.

MISS READ

EARLY DAYS

ILLUSTRATIONS BY DEREK CROWE

PENGUIN BOOKS

PENGUIN BOOKS

Published by the Penguin Group
Penguin Books Ltd, 27 Wrights Lane, London W8 5TZ, England
Penguin Books USA Inc., 375 Hudson Street, New York, New York 10014, USA
Penguin Books Australia Ltd, Ringwood, Victoria, Australia
Penguin Books Canada Ltd, 10 Alcorn Avenue, Toronto, Ontario, Canada M4V 3B2
Penguin Books (NZ) Ltd, 182–190 Wairau Road, Auckland 10, New Zealand

Penguin Books Ltd, Registered Offices: Harmondsworth, Middlesex, England

A Fortunate Grandchild first published by Michael Joseph 1982
Time Remembered first published by Michael Joseph 1986
First published in one volume with a new foreword by Michael Joseph 1995
First published in Penguin Books 1996
1 3 5 7 9 10 8 6 4 2

A Fortunate Grandchild text copyright © Miss Read, 1982
Illustrations copyright © Derek Crowe, 1982
Time Remembered text copyright © Miss Read, 1986
Illustrations copyright © Derek Crowe, 1982
Foreword copyright © Miss Read, 1995
All rights reserved

The moral right of the author has been asserted

Printed in England by Clays Ltd, St Ives plc

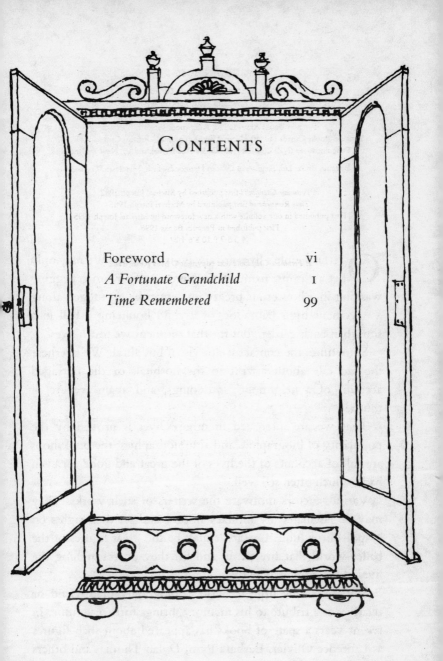

Contents

Foreword   vi
A Fortunate Grandchild   1
Time Remembered   99

FOREWORD

O THER people's lives are always interesting. We may only
get a glimpse from a train window of a woman pegging
washing in a boisterous breeze, or a man being tugged along
a pavement by a Labrador, or a child bouncing a ball in a
suburban back garden, but for that moment we touch lives.

Sometimes the contact is not visual but aural. We overhear
the sad tale about a visit to the hospital, or the outraged
account of a neighbour's misdoings, and again we are in
touch.

That we are interested in others' lives is proved by the
popularity of biographies and autobiographies: the bookshops
are full of accounts of the lives of the great and good (or even
bad), which often sell well.

Various factors motivate the writers of such works. They
may be fascinated by military history and set their sights on
Napoleon or Julius Caesar. It may be the great figures of the
ballet world that fire them, and off they go researching the
lives of Nijinsky or Pavlova.

Sometimes the urge to write a biography of a friend or
relative, as a tribute to his memory, brings forth a volume. In
recent years a spate of books has appeared about such figures
as Laurence Olivier, Barbara Pym, Dylan Thomas and others
who have died.

Money, of course, is a constant motive. Quite a number, one suspects, look up the anniversaries of interesting people, well in advance, and buckle down to getting a biography to their publisher before others do so. Money can, too, motivate those who have attained eminence in their lifetimes to write their autobiographies (which are often, like biographies, large and heavy tomes, despite the fact that the finished product is too unwieldy to read in bed).

But a great many autobiographies are written by less well-known people and for a far simpler reason. They want to tell their families, and particularly those who follow after them, how things were when the writer was young, and what happened to that writer later.

A great many of these modest accounts never reach the publisher's office, let alone the bookshops, but they have intrinsic value for the writer and reader. There is a lasting fascination with the world which one has just missed, one's mother's memories and one's grandmother's too, such as the fact that my own Grandma Read was married in a wedding dress, presumably homemade, which 'cost six-three a yard', as she boasted. (That means it cost sixpence and three farthings in the money of that day, and about three pence a yard in ours.) And, as you will read, she wore 'an aerofane bonnet with gooseberries on it', with this creation.

This change in the value of money is one of the strongest factors of our interest in times past. Like many people of my generation I was irritated by my parents' constant mention of how much a sovereign, a real one made of gold and kept in a velvet-lined sovereign case, would buy 'before the war'. By this they meant the war of 1914–1918 which devastated their lives.

It was brought home to me later by our own daughter, then aged about six in the 1940s, who picked up something from the kitchen table, maybe an Oxo cube or a custard packet, and remarked in wonder:

'Can you really *buy* something for a penny?'

A penny, at her age, would have been riches for me.

It is this word-of-mouth communication between the generations which makes social history so vivid, and so vital.

It was mainly for her interest, and for readers of her generation and after, that I wrote the two accounts of my childhood. For the first seven years I was a London child and in close touch with my maternal grandmother and a bevy of uncles, aunts and cousins. *A Fortunate Grandchild* covers this period.

There was still a hint of Victorian times about the London of my very early years. The muffin man walked the winter streets with his wares balanced in a tray on his head, and a brass handbell to advertise them. The lamp-lighter cycled from lamp-post to lamp-post as dusk fell. And all the women had skirts that swept to the ground.

But at the age of seven I was taken to live in the country, and the impact this made has coloured my life ever since. *Time Remembered* was written to record the bliss of this time, ending with my transfer to a large girls' school at the age of eleven.

I am sometimes asked if I intend to continue with my autobiography, and the answer is 'No', for two reasons.

As a reader of other writers' autobiographies it is always the early years which I enjoy most, and I believe this is fairly general. There is a freshness, a lightness, about these early memories which often fades as the author grows to manhood and we follow his path to fame.

The second reason for deciding to end my own recollections at the age of eleven is even simpler. Like most people, my early memories are sharp. I could take you today to the spot where I found violets, or a robin's nest, seventy years ago, but I should be hard put to it to tell you where I left my spectacles ten minutes ago, or what I was doing on Thursday of last week. That is why I pray that I shall never be called as a witness in a court of law. Memory becomes blurred and inaccurate as time passes, and the incidents of my twenties and thirties would not have the clarity of those early days.

Some of the most enchanting contributions to English literature have been childhood memories, of course. Gwen Raverat's *Period Piece*, Flora Thompson's *Lark Rise to Candleford* and, recently, Dirk Bogarde's *Great Meadow* come to mind. They are perfect examples of the powerful impact the world makes upon a young mind. Those first impressions are sharp and clear upon the virgin page. Gradually the dust of years will settle upon it, blurring what follows. But if the dust is blown away, those first marks will still show vividly throughout one's life.

One aspect of these two autobiographical essays only struck me recently when I re-read them for this edition. It was how true we are to our beginnings, and Wordsworth's phrase '*The Child is father of the Man*' was recalled with great force. The dislike of crowds and loud noises is still with me, and I remember how I hated going to a certain greengrocer's with my mother when I was about four years old. It was always busy, people shoved and shouted, and the man who was selling his wares made more noise than the rest put together.

Children's parties too I found overwhelming. The shrieks, the laughter, the general hubbub were not to my taste. Looking back, I see now, that even then I was a ruminatory animal (as writers need to be), and was exhausted rather than exhilarated by a crowd of boisterous people.

Railway stations, with steam trains in those days, and another crush of people, were also terrifying. Occasional visits to the street markets of Petticoat Lane and the Caledonian Market were a pleasure to my mother and aunts, but not to me being tugged along reluctantly behind.

Another unpleasant experience, shared with my sister, was having to perform in public. In those days, children were expected to contribute to family entertainment by reciting, singing or playing 'a piano piece'. Squirming with embarassment we would go through our paces, and resume our chairs with relief. Even now I dislike hearing my work read on radio, or to a live audience, though, unaccountably, I feel a glow of pride when I see the books displayed in the bookseller's.

But happier aspects of my childhood remain constant. I get the same thrill today as I did then, if I come across a rare wild flower such as a bee orchid, or catch a glimpse of a woodpecker or a kingfisher. When Wordsworth said:

> *My heart leaps up when I behold*
> *A rainbow in the sky,*

we may feel that the sentiment is a little exaggerated, but we all know exactly what he means.

Another influence upon those of my generation was the Great War, as it was then called. Its shadow hung chillingly over our childhood, no matter how bravely the adults tried to shelter us from it. We were brought up in a mainly female world while the men fought far from home. Food was in short supply and we London children anyway knew air raids first-hand. We recognized sorrow too on the faces of aunts and uncles, both kindred and adopted, when bad news had arrived, and we saw the limping men in hospital blue struggling about the streets.

It is these early memories, I believe, which make my generation deeply moved by the poetry written at that time and, perhaps more than most, we feel such desolation when coming across those heartrendingly long lists of names on the walls of churches, chapels, colleges, schools and village war memorials commemorating the illustrious dead.

Earlier I mentioned that one of the pleasures of reading autobiographies is the emergence of the grown character and his attainments.

Although I have not written about my adult years, and do not intend to in book form, it may be of interest to readers, and even more so to incipient writers, to give a brief account of what befell me after the age of eleven when I left my beloved village school in Kent.

My career at Bromley County School was undistinguished, and by the time I was due to leave at the age of eighteen, I only knew vaguely that I should like a job with books, and that I should like to write. My parents sensibly suggested that I should spent two years training to be a teacher, collect some qualification which would support me throughout life, if need be, and do any writing in my spare time.

This project was heartily endorsed by my Aunt Rose, herself a competent infants' teacher, and I went off to Homerton College, Cambridge, where I made several dear and lifelong friends, and fell in love with the city of Cambridge.

The grace and diversity of the university's buildings, complemented by the market town atmosphere, delighted me.

An even more powerful influence was the River Cam. Brought up on the windy heights of the North Downs, I knew little of rivers and their joys. The mighty Thames I knew well, of course, but I had never before come across a river that ran, small and friendly, right through a town, creating its own swathe of beauty.

The Cambridgeshire countryside was a complete contrast to my native Kentish landscape. I liked its flatness, its enormous skies, and farther north the austere beauty of the Fens in winter.

My horizons were broadened, in the literal sense, and when I went to a college friend's home and was introduced to the Lake District, I realized how deeply moved I was by all the diversity to be found in even such a small country as England.

After two years in Cambridge I went to Middlesex to teach in a large new school. Within a few years war arrived in September 1939. I married in the following year and went to live in Witney, Oxfordshire, where our daughter was born and where I discovered the charm of yet another area, the Cotswolds.

This appreciation of my surroundings has always been a vital contribution to my life and later to my writings. At the northern end of Witney is Wood Green, and this was the setting for the Thrush Green novels which I wrote some twenty years later.

After the war we moved to the Newbury area where my husband returned to his teaching post at St Bartholomew's Grammar School.

We lived in a nearby village for some years, and later to our present home over thirty years ago. Our daughter lives and works in the adjoining county of Oxfordshire, only a few miles from her birthplace.

I also did short spells of teaching in local village schools and started my writing career by sending work to various journals such as *The Times Educational Supplement* and *Punch*. (A collection of these light essays, or short stories, has recently been published under the title *Tales from a Village School*).

In 1955 my first book was published by Michael Joseph and Penguin and since then they have taken one a year, so I have been busy ever since.

Whenever I start a book it is the *place* which comes first and the *people* second. I like to have the setting clear in my mind before I set the actors to work upon the stage. To most novelists, I believe, their work can be construed as 'Figures in a Landscape'. My novels tend to be 'A Landscape with Figures'. Luckily, readers seem to like it that way.

So many people intend to write down their memories, and to all those would-be autobiographers, I venture to give this advice. Do the job for your own enjoyment and for the sake of those who come after you. You will be providing a valuable social contribution whether it finds a publisher or not. Some of those which I have enjoyed most have been printed privately and given enormous pleasure to family and friends.

It is not an easy task, but it becomes more absorbing as the memories start to flow, and for those who have had the foresight to keep diaries, the outcome is infinitely more accurate, of course.

You hold my effort in your hands, and if it does nothing more, I trust that it will stir early memories and encourage you, perhaps, to set down your own.

A
FORTUNATE
GRANDCHILD

Contents

Author's Note   4

My Two Grandmothers   7

Grandma Read   9
Aunt Jess   18
Aunt Rose   25
Uncle Harry   36
267 Hither Green Lane   40
A Sad Ending   52

Grandma Shafe   55
Summer 1914   61
Grandpa Shafe   65
The Beach Hut   70
An Outing with Grandma   74
Going to Grandma's   77
17 New Pier Street   85
Holiday Rituals   91
Long-lost Relatives   94
The Last Years   96

Author's Note

I AM much indebted to my sister who confirmed or amended a number of these memories.

I should like to thank also my cousin Doris Shafe and Reginald Davies who supplied the photographs of our grand-mothers and some happy recollections.

Most of the events recorded happened some sixty or more years ago, and I am conscious that there may be errors. For these I claim full responsibility, and hope that they may be forgiven.

To
Those Who Shared
My Two Grandmothers

My sister Lil aged four, and me aged sixteen months, in the summer of 1914

MY TWO GRANDMOTHERS

I WAS lucky with my grandmothers. Both Grandma Read and Grandma Shafe were dears.

I was not so lucky with grandfathers. One had died years before I was born, and Thomas Smith Shafe was as daunting to a child as his jolly wife was welcoming.

Speaking generally, it seems to me that grandmothers have a very special place in the affections of young children. Not obliged, as parents are, to provide food, shelter, protection, advice and discipline, day in and day out, they can afford to be much more easy-going. The unexpected present, the extra outing, the little treat of a favourite meal prepared especially to delight the child and, above all, the time to listen to youthful outpourings, all make a grandmother a loved ally. It is hardly surprising that the bond between grandmother and grandchild is often stronger than that between parent and child.

My own two grandmothers were alike in the affection they so freely bestowed, and the love they inspired. They were quite different in looks, one small and dark, the other large – *very* large – with curly white hair. One had borne twelve children, the other four. Grandma Read was the widow of a Deptford builder. Grandma Shafe's husband Tom was a retired Post Office worker. More of him anon, for although he does not play a large role in this account of my two grandmothers, he nevertheless made his presence felt at 17 New Pier Street, Walton-on-Naze, where they went to live when he retired.

But it is Grandma Read of 267 Hither Green Lane, Lewisham, that I remember most vividly when I was a very young child, and I will describe her, her family and her home first.

GRANDMA READ

Sarah Ann Read
1846–1922

GRANDMA READ

SHE was my mother's mother and must have been nearly seventy when I first became conscious of her in about 1915. At that time, my father was serving in France with H Battery of the Royal Horse Artillery, and my mother was carrying on his job as an insurance agent. My elder sister and I were left with Grandma Read, who lived near by, for most of the day.

She was small and neat, with a very smooth skin and dark hair parted in the middle and taken back behind her ears into a bun. Her hair remained dark and glossy until her death at seventy-six. It was generally believed that she had a Portuguese forbear and her looks would certainly bear this out.

She dressed well. Her frocks were of dark silk, usually brown or black, trimmed with lace and made with a high neck. She was particularly fond of prettily-trimmed bonnets worn tied under the chin with ribbons. As children, we often gave her bonnet trimmings of feathers or velvet for her birthday or Christmas presents. One particular bonnet I remember clearly, trimmed with velvet pansies of different colours which framed her face and delighted my admiring eye.

An older cousin of mine remembers her as 'a very happy lady. She had a nice smile, and her eyes smiled too.' That too is how I remember her.

She was a wonderful companion to young children, cheerful, spritely and not over-anxious, as so many adults are, about the niceties of correct behaviour or the awful consequences of such daring feats as jumping off low walls or down the conservatory steps. Having had twelve children of her own, she was probably past worrying over much.

She indulged me in small ways, and I loved her for it.

During that war, food supplies were extremely short, especially in London. My mother had instilled in us that we were never to ask for sweets or anything with sugar in it because people had so little. My grandmother, however, would frequently spread butter – or more probably margarine in those days – on half a slice of bread, and then scatter brown sugar on it. I watched greedily as she cut it into fingers which I soon demolished. I knew, as well as she did, that this activity was only undertaken when we were alone, and I had enough sense, even at three, to keep our secret.

Twice a week Grandma Read left her house to walk a few hundred yards to a small cinema. She adored films – black and white and silent, of course – and rarely missed one. They were changed twice a week, and Grandma returned from her outings much refreshed. Sometimes she was accompanied by one of my aunts or a cousin, but she was perfectly happy to go alone. Charlie Chaplin, Pearl White, Mary Pickford and all the rest, provided her with exciting enough company.

St Swithun's church a little farther along the road was the family's parish church. I cannot remember if my grandmother was a regular member of the congregation but my two aunts, Rose and Jess, certainly were, and clergymen, choirboys and other church members often came back after the service to

267 Hither Green Lane for refreshments, and to sing round the piano in Grandma's drawing-room. My sister, three years older than I am, was as bored as I was on these occasions, and it was she who showed me how delightful it was to creep behind the piano, and sit there among piles of sheet music in comparative peace.

Of the twelve children born to my grandmother, eight survived, which was not a bad percentage in those days. The

date of her marriage I do not know, but probably about the mid-sixties of the last century. She told her children that her wedding dress was much admired, and that she wore 'an aerophane bonnet with gooseberries on it'. What aerophane was nobody knew, but the unintentional couplet is unforgettable. Queen Victoria was on the throne from the time of Grandma's birth until she was in her fifties. It was not a very healthy time for babies or their mothers, and I suppose that to have eight out of twelve living to maturity was not bad going.

The first child, my uncle George, I never knew. He had emigrated to Australia, married there and had children, one of whom was called Harlene. As this was also the name of a hair tonic of that time, the family found it an odd choice. I don't think Grandma heard from him very often.

My aunts Liz and Nell were married with children, and my mother, the last but one of this long family, had produced my sister Lil and me. Another sister, Betty, was born much later, in 1927.

Of the remaining boys, my Uncle Chris was married but

he and my Aunt Maud were childless. The three unmarried children, my Aunt Jess, Aunt Rose and Uncle Harry, lived at home with my grandmother, so that the house was always busy and there always seemed to be someone free to take an interest in one's pleasures.

I knew all the Beatrix Potter stories before I started school, thanks to one or other of the aunts who always seemed to be able to spare time to read them to us. They also sang to us, as did my mother (it was a great family for singing). As well as the more obvious nursery rhymes such as 'Ring-a-ring-of-roses', we rejoiced in such roistering music hall numbers as:

> Joshua, Joshua,
> Nicer than lemon squash you are!
> You'll be pleased to know
> You are my best beau!

(Naturally, I thought this had some obscure connection with my hair ribbon.)

Or, rendered at a terrific pace:

> Any old iron? Any old iron?
> Any any any old iron?
> You look sweet, just a treat,
> You look a daisy
> From your napper to your feet.

We sang too, unconscious of their poignancy, the contemporary war-time songs such as:

Goodbye-ee, Goodbye-ee
Wipe the tear, baby dear,
From your eye-ee!
It is hard to part I know,
But I'll be tickled to death to go!

In the great cupboard under the kitchen dresser, Grandma had two wooden grooved butter pats, and these she would give me with a large lump of plasticine. Bashing happily, I tried to emulate the deft strokes of the grocer at the local Home and Colonial Stores who slapped up pounds of butter and margarine on a marble slab, ending up with beautiful striped oblongs. Mine were less symmetrical, and the din must have been prodigious, but I cannot remember anyone objecting in that indulgent household.

Another object which I admired in the kitchen was a pin cushion in the shape of a Chinese doll. It had a round head with a pigtail, and its stuffed body was made of dark red satin. It was occasionally lifted down from its peg by the mantelpiece for me to hold, but I was not allowed to play with it in case the pins and needles, with which it bristled, scratched me. No doubt, the aunts and Grandma also envisaged me swallowing some. In any case, after a brief period of admiration, it was returned to safety.

Never did I feel that I was a nuisance, as I must have been quite often and, looking back, I realize that it was Aunt Jess who bore the brunt of my relentless attentions. She deserves a few pages to herself.

AUNT JESS

MY AUNT JESS, the youngest of the brood, was virtually housekeeper and general dogsbody. I loved her dearly. She was small in stature, rather skinny, and had dark hair which she frizzed with hair tongs heated in the fishtail flame of the gas bracket in the bedroom. I watched this operation with great interest. The smell of singed hair was alarming. Would my Aunt Jess go up in smoke? Nevertheless, I much admired the semi-Afro fringe which resulted.

When she took off her gold pince-nez, her eyes looked weak and as though they belonged to someone else. The look frightened me, as much as the dreadful concentrated look of my mother as she threaded a needle. Perhaps it was the complete withdrawal into another realm which shook me. I only know that I was relieved when Aunt Jess replaced her glasses, which made a cruel red indentation on each side of her slightly snub nose, and my mother succeeded in threading the needle, and both returned to me.

Aunt Jess had been trained as a dressmaker, and at the top of the house was her small workroom. Here there were the most fascinating objects.

A large model figure encased in shiny sateen dominated the room. From the hips down was a wire cage, but above that the great swelling bust billowed out regally from the wasp waist. The whole thing was topped by a shiny wooden knob where the neck should be. Aunt Jess referred to this inanimate companion as 'Arabella', and always seemed to be hovering around her, with her mouth full of pins, as she draped material over that exuberant bust.

Aunt Jess also had the miniature clothes which she had made when she had learnt her craft. These miracles of feather-stitching, tucking, hemming, smocking and so on, were mounted on cardboard and we were not allowed to touch them. There was a long work bench, covered in black oil cloth, much scratched by scissors, pins and other tools of the trade. I remember adding to the scars by trundling an object with a little wheel up and down the surface. It left a fascinating row of pin-pricks, but a slap on the hand put a stop to this pleasant pastime.

Of course, there were drifts of tissue paper patterns, and transfers in blue print on flimsy paper depicting unlikely flowers, garlands and geometrical edgings. There was also a delicious substance called, I believe, tailor's chalk, which was flat and shiny, and used for marking material. Sometimes, Aunt Jess would give me a broken piece. If licked, it clung to one's lips rather disconcertingly. It drew beautifully though on pieces of brown paper, spread flat on the kitchen floor, ready for my artistic efforts later in the day.

In this minute room, Aunt Jess fitted her clients' clothes. I don't know if she had many customers, but she certainly had very little time for this particular pursuit. She did most of the cooking, house-cleaning and laundry work, for I cannot remember any help in the house, and it was a fairly large one to keep clean.

She also made a good many clothes for the family, and I can remember several of the things she made for us as children. My sister and I were resplendent in black and white check coats, with black velvet collars, at one stage. I had a white muff on a cord round my neck with this rig-out. Whether Lil also sported one, I cannot recall, but if she objected, I have no doubt she was spared. She was a strong-minded child.

Aunt Jess also concocted green velvet frocks for us with curious tabs round the waist, somewhat reminiscent of mediaeval tunic decorations — a late-flowering of the pre-Raphaelite influence, perhaps? Each tab was decorated with an embossed pink rose, and I can't think that a row of these round that portion of our anatomies, hopefully known as our waists, could have done anything for us. She also made us cream delaine pinafore frocks. I wore a pink-sprigged blouse with mine, and Lil a blue.

Much later, she made me a white voile frock for my confirmation. It had a lace insertion down the front, and lace endings at neck and cuffs. I loathed it, and no doubt poor Aunt Jess was not thanked properly for it. I was much nicer at three than thirteen.

I can remember a splendid evening cloak she made for my mother for some forgotten function when the war was over. It was of bronze satin, lined with peach satin, and had large buttons covered with the same brown material. My Aunt Rose, who deserves, and will get, a few pages to herself, had painted each button with a little sprig of pink flowers, and the whole effect was stunning. All this work, on delicate or heavy materials, was done on Aunt Jess's Frister-Rossman sewing machine. This was a fine German instrument, and could either be worked by turning a handle or by a foot treadle.

I wonder now how Aunt Jess could have done such fine work for her hands were always rough and chapped from housework. The cleaning materials of some sixty odd years ago were pretty fierce. Soda, Monkey Brand, strong yellow soap cut in thick chunks from a long heavy bar of the stuff, using the kitchen coal shovel to get plenty of 'purchase' on it, hearth-stone for the door steps, and Brasso for knockers, finger-plates and door-knobs, all took their toll on human skin, and a little Pond's cold cream was probably all that Aunt Jess's hard-working hands ever received. No doubt, she was too whacked at night even to bother with that.

Looking back, I wonder that Aunt Jess

never married. It is true that she was no beauty, but many plainer women have found husbands. She had a sweet disposition and was unfailingly kind. When some years later, my mother was seriously ill, it was Aunt Jess who came to hold the fort. When my younger sister was born, it was again Aunt Jess who ran the house.

She never seemed to sit down and have a real rest. I used to dog her footsteps, up the interminable flights of stairs, or down into the terrifying cellar which ran beneath the hall and out under the front garden path. Near the cellar door was a small cupboard where newspapers were stored for lighting fires, together with bundles of kindling wood.

One day, close at Aunt Jess's heels, I watched her pulling out paper and wood, hurrying as usual, puffing slightly as she rushed from one job to the next, when she dropped her armful with a dreadful squeal, yelping: 'A mouse! A mouse!'

Shuddering, she fled to the kitchen. I looked into the murk of the paper cupboard, but the mouse had vanished. Disappointed, I returned to Aunt Jess.

Now, I am ashamed to say, I react with as much horror to an intruding mouse as dear Aunt Jess.

Although she was always busy, she found time to read, as I have said, such delectable works as *The Tale of Mrs Tittlemouse* and *The Tale of Benjamin Bunny* to us. And I can remember a favourite game of mine which she played with me whilst she was ironing or stirring a pot on the kitchen range.

The game was simple, called 'Shopping'. Armed with a basket, I asked my busy aunt for such things as Sunlight soap, cocoa, a loaf of bread and other such basic necessities which were still procurable in war time. With a wave of her one free hand, she would deposit the invisible goods in my basket and I would pay her with bone counters.

The delicious climax came when I requested 'A farthing's-worth of currants'. At this, my indulgent aunt would cease her task for a minute and reach up to a high kitchen shelf where stood a row of metal canisters. From one, she shook into my fat palm a few precious currants. I handed over my counter-farthing, and the game ended in blissful nibbling.

I realize now how much Aunt Jess meant to that household at 267 Hither Green Lane. She was Grandma Read's right hand (for the other two unmarried inhabitants, Aunt Rose and Uncle Harry, were out at work), and an amazingly good aunt to the many children of the family who came to stay.

She was also my godmother as well as my aunt, and I am glad that my parents gave me my second name, Jessie, as a tribute to her.

AUNT ROSE

M Y AUNT ROSE must have been ten or more years older than Aunt Jess, and was quite a different kettle of fish. Grandma Read seemed to defer rather more to Aunt Rose's judgement than to Aunt Jess's.

Aunt Rose was small and dark, but plumper and decidedly more handsome than Aunt Jess. She had masses of glossy dark brown hair, always beautifully dressed, a fine complexion which she tended with *papier poudré* leaflets torn from a tiny booklet kept in her handbag, and very bright dark eyes like her mother's. She dressed well, and wore a good many brooches and beads.

She taught at Ennersdale Road School nearby and I have no doubt, knowing now some of the qualities needed to make a sound infants' teacher, that Aunt Rose was an exceptionally competent one. Her manner was motherly, but brisk and firm. Her standards of behaviour were high, and she would have brooked no laziness.

She was blessed too with those accomplishments most needed for infant work. She was artistic and very skilled with her hands. Grandma's drawing-room had several of her watercolours on the walls, and she worked indefatigably at such ploys as pen-painting, crochet and something called, I believe, pastenalla work. This latter involved painting such objects as kingfishers perched on bulrushes, or sprays of flowers, on to black velvet or satin, and then spraying them with minute glassy balls. The result was a shiny picture, and many a cushion cover, table runner, and evening bag were pressed upon reluctant recipients. My sister and I, as we grew older, deplored Aunt Rose's taste and her industry, and were particularly difficult about some velvet hair bands ornamented with roses which my mother insisted on our wearing, 'at least once', to please her older sister.

She must have found great consolation in such projects as classroom friezes, pasting pictures on screens, book jackets and making calendars, Christmas and Easter cards, paper windmills, artificial flowers and all the other endless forms of handwork undertaken in the infants' class. There must be many of her pupils who remember Aunt Rose with affection, and owe their basic grounding in handwork, reading, writing and arithmetic to her sound teaching.

She was a determined woman. Later, I heard just how tenaciously she had persisted in taking up her teaching career.

Evidently she had served several years as a pupil-teacher before deciding that she must qualify as a certificated teacher. For this she needed to take a teachers' training course. In those days, this needed money which Aunt Rose did not have. Grandma Read, although approving of Rose's ambitions, simply had no idea how to set about helping her.

With commendable courage, Aunt Rose went to an uncle of hers who was rather better off than the rest of the family, and put the problem to him. He nobly stumped up. Aunt Rose promised to repay him as soon as she had a teaching job, and before long she was a student at Brighton Training College, where I have no doubt she did extremely well.

It was Aunt Rose who took me first to school with her. This must have been in 1917 on April 16th, as I know that my fourth birthday was the next day. My clever elder sister was already steaming ahead on the second floor of the great L.C.C. building in 'the Big Girls'' department. I was deposited in the babies' class, not Aunt Rose's, and given a box of china beads to thread, whilst admiring the magnificent rocking-horse and making plans for an early ride.

My hopes were dashed by the

afternoon when it was discovered that I could read. I was wrenched from my beads and the rocking-horse and pushed up one standard where I had to work quite hard. Aunt Rose was delighted.

I was not.

Although Grandma Read was undoubtedly the head of her household, and she was deferred to by all those in it, I have no doubt that Aunt Rose played a large part in its running. She had plenty of business sense, and would have been capable of coping with household accounts and such matters as insurance, leases, rates and other domestic and financial affairs.

I suspect, too, that her salary was a major part of the family's income, and she would see it was wisely spent. Not that she was mean. Although she dressed well, and always appeared with good shoes, handbags and hats, she was generous with her presents to her nieces and nephews, and gave us all some splendid books – interspersed, of course, with the regrettable hair bands, belts and collars of her own making – and I still use *Tales From Shakespeare* by Charles and Mary Lamb, published by Ward Lock, and ablaze with beautiful coloured plates and inscribed in Aunt Rose's hand:

To Dear Little Dora, with love.

It was a present for my ninth birthday.

As well as spending her money on books for us, both she and Aunt Jess were generous in taking us to the theatre as soon as we were old enough to enjoy it. We saw all the Aldwych farces with Tom Walls and Ralph Lynn, and Mary Brough of blessed memory, as well as *No, No, Nanette* and other light musicals which appealed to my aunts. We were also taken to a lavishly-produced version of *A Midsummer Night's Dream*, complete with a slowly-breaking dawn, gauzy fairies, Mendelssohn's music and the most ravishing costumes and sets. This was in the early 1920s, and may have been the Max Reinhart production. It certainly impressed us.

Looking back, I can see that Aunt Rose's dominance in the household must have been irksome at times to her youngest sister, Aunt Jess. Grandma Read, I imagine, was able to ignore, or even be mildly amused by, Rose's 'bossiness'. Aunt Jess would have had to endure it rather more directly and, some years later, after Grandma Read's death, she and Uncle Harry together with an older sister Lizzie, set up house together, while Rose bought a comfortable house not far from Hither Green Lane which she converted into two very pleasant flats, one for her own use and the other to let to well-vetted tenants.

Aunt Rose was certainly the best-looking, best-dressed and probably the most intelligent of Grandma's daughters. She never married, although she had a steady admirer and they remained devoted for many years.

Her manner with men was somewhat flirtatious and affected, and my father, who was a cheerfully irreverent man, took great delight in teasing her. As we grew older, my sister and I were embarrassed by her affected ways, and naughtily amused by the dark hints she gave about 'what might have been'.

I well remember walking home with her after seeing *The Student Prince* and remarking that it was a pity that he married the wrong girl in the end. The hero's sense of duty – I was about ten at the time – seemed misplaced to me.

'Ah!' said Aunt Rose, sighing heavily into the darkness. 'Life Is Like That! One has to put one's duty to others before one's own pleasures.'

And then followed several remarks which might have been construed as Aunt Rose's personal renunciation of passionate love and blissful marriage, in order to maintain the household at 267. But, there again, it may just have been the aftermath of seeing *The Student Prince* late one night at the Lewisham Hippodrome.

★

As far as I can judge at this distance of time, she took her religion, orthodox Church of England, very seriously. She went regularly to St Swithun's church, and I have no doubt that much of her handwork went into the appreciative channels of church bazaars.

She also ran the Sunday School attached to this church, although one might have thought that she saw quite enough of young children during the rest of the week.

She organized the session admirably. Simple hymns and prayers alternated with handwork, making Moses in plasticine, for instance, to put into a carefully woven cradle and hidden among dried sticks erected in a sand tray. There was quite a bit of marching, if I remember correctly, when we put our collection money into a box, whilst we sang:

> See the farthings dropping,
> Listen as they fall

or something very similar.

The whole programme was conducted with great skill and gusto by Aunt Rose, and I think she played the piano as well.

Later, she and a friend, Miss Hetty Lee, collaborated on a useful manual for Sunday School teachers called *Little Children of the Church*, which incorporated these ideas, and gave appropriate lessons and practical work for every Sunday in the year, thus giving small children a basic understanding of the great church festivals and the pattern of the Christian year. It was in print for many years.

Aunt Rose's organizing ability was also to the fore in helping to arrange the mammoth Fancy Dress Party which was held annually at Goldsmiths' College, New Cross, I suppose it was in aid of some deserving cause. My sister and I,

never great ones for pleasure *en masse*, rather dreaded these occasions when we were tricked out as shepherdesses, or nursery rhyme characters, in costumes made by my hard-pressed Aunt Jess. I heartily loathed all my regalia on these occasions, and pined to go as a powder-puff, with a fetching

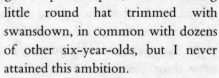

little round hat trimmed with swansdown, in common with dozens of other six-year-olds, but I never attained this ambition.

The nadir of the evening, in our eyes, was the Grand Parade when we marched two by two round and round the enormous hall, surveyed by fond parents and the judges on the stage. Aunt Rose, aglow with pearls and satin, beamed proudly upon us as we passed.

The refreshments were always superb, and I rather think we were all given a present at the end of the evening.

Even so, we were jolly glad it was all over for another year.

A certain amount of entertaining was done under Grandma Read's roof, and I think Aunt Rose instigated much of it. I can remember a number of young soldiers, usually connected in some way with St Swithun's, enjoying tea there. From one, when I was three, I received my first proposal of marriage – or at least, 'an understanding' – but he was one of the many who never returned. His name was Reveley Brown, although this spelling is phonetic, as I never saw it written. Another young soldier married an older cousin.

Sometimes one or two of the clergy came to 267, and a frequent visitor was an old sailor called Maskell, who had been with Peary on his Arctic expedition early in the century. I imagine that some of Aunt Rose's teaching colleagues also visited the house, but I do not remember seeing them. No doubt I was then abed.

The journey to school, at least in the early days, always seems to have had Aunt Rose as a guardian angel.

I was glad of this for several reasons. Quite often we saw 'the cats' meat man', who drove a little gig in which were numberless wooden skewers threaded with slices of cooked horse meat. He had a raucous voice to advertise his wares, and cat owners would run out with their pennies. Naturally, the cats came too when they heard the welcome cries.

I adored cats, and still do, and for some unaccountable reason I thought 'a cats' meat man' collected the cats, killed and cooked them, and loaded his wooden skewers so that he

could entice more to their brothers' gruesome feast. No doubt someone told me that the provender was horseflesh, and I had not listened or, more likely, I never confessed my awful anxieties on behalf of the trusting cats which followed the little cart. It was good to have Aunt Rose's hand to hold.

There was also a railway bridge across the road we traversed, and the rumbling of trains overhead terrified me. It was only a matter of time, I felt sure, before one fell through the bridge and engulfed us all in a horrifying chaos.

Quite a number of bombs fell in that part of London in the First World War. 'Aiming for Woolwich Arsenal,' said the know-alls. I certainly recall passing a great crater in St Swithun's churchyard after a night raid, and the piles of sandbags round the school walls to protect us from the blast. We were too young to be frightened much, but it was a comfort to have Aunt Rose's company.

She remained the lynch-pin of the family for many years. No wedding, funeral or other function was complete without Aunt Rose to the fore.

Despite her little affectations, which irritated us inordinately as we grew into our teens, she was an admirable woman, hard-working, shrewd, bountifully fond of children and interested in everything.

She long out-lived her younger sisters, and was in her eighties when she died.

UNCLE HARRY

M Y UNCLE HARRY, though resident at Grandma Read's, lived in a world of his own. I don't think that I have ever met anyone quite so dreamily abstracted as this diminutive uncle.

It was G. K. Chesterton, I think, who pointed out that absence of mind meant presence of mind elsewhere. This was so, I imagine, in Uncle Harry's case.

He was absorbed in two subjects. The Young Men's Christian Association was one, and some sect which believed that the future was foretold by the hieroglyphics on the Pyramids. The tribes of Israel also figured in this doctrine, and Uncle Harry was a dedicated believer.

His job was something to do with the newspaper world, on the printing side. He went daily to Fleet Street as far as I

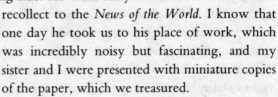

recollect to the *News of the World*. I know that one day he took us to his place of work, which was incredibly noisy but fascinating, and my sister and I were presented with miniature copies of the paper, which we treasured.

I suppose that he had some modest routine job which he accomplished quite satisfactorily as he was never sacked, and which enabled his mind to rove happily over the two subjects dearest to his heart.

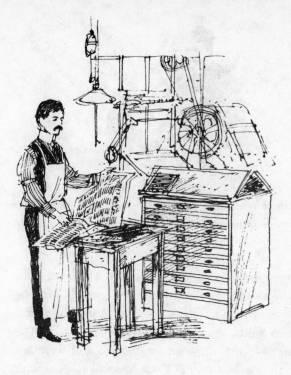

He was a tiny man with brown dreamy eyes, and an enormous walrus moustache. We hated receiving Uncle Harry's damp and fumbling kisses and did our best to dodge them, although our mischievous father inevitably prompted us to our reluctantly undertaken duty. Left alone, I don't think Uncle Harry would have noticed our presence, and the part he played in my Grandma's house was a minor one.

However, when pressed at family parties, he was public-spirited enough to sing 'Little Annie Rooney', his one party piece, after Aunt Rose had obliged with 'Hark, Hark the Lark' in a tremulous soprano. (As girls, my sister and I mimicked Aunt Rose in action. Now, I confess, I sound exactly the same when I take to song.)

Uncle Harry wore neat dark suits, but what I found most intriguing were elastic armbands made of metal which he wore above his elbows over his shirt sleeves. I suppose it was difficult for such a little man to buy small enough shirts. The armbands were snapped off when he changed and were left on the dressing-table. Sometimes I was allowed to play with them in Uncle Harry's absence. No doubt he had forgotten to put them on on these happy occasions.

He was a tireless worker for the local branch of the Y.M.C.A. and I remember going to a fête to raise funds for

this good cause. The chief attraction to me was a wooden bust of a negro at the entrance. He was holding out a black hand on which one put a coin. Immediately, the hand came up to the widely grinning mouth and the coin was gulped down. I badgered Uncle Harry until he showed me the lever at the back which controlled

this miracle. I have had a soft spot for the Y.M.C.A. ever since.

He had a small bedroom on the first floor of 267 overlooking the garden. It was very plain and neat – kept so, I have no doubt, by hardworking Aunt Jess – and the only ornament that I can remember was a china bust of a jester in cap and bells.

This little figurine was reversible. On one side the jester leant back, the silent bells shaken back from his laughing face, a picture of well-fed happiness. On the reverse side, the bells hung around a doleful face with pursed mouth and many wrinkles. I coveted this ornament, but was only allowed to hold it occasionally, and then over Uncle Harry's white counterpane 'in case it broke'.

Grandma Read, and the rest of the family, seemed to treat Uncle Harry with the tender indulgence given to a backward child. I doubt if he was ever asked to undertake any matter of responsibility, in case he forgot it. On the other hand, despite his apparent vagueness, he was no fool, and when finally he became the one man in the household which was set up with Aunt Jess and Aunt Lizzie, after Grandma's death, he probably emerged as a much more capable man than he had appeared when over-protected by his mother, Aunt Jess and Aunt Rose.

267 HITHER GREEN LANE

I F UNCLE HARRY'S room made little impression on a young
child, apart from the china jester and the occasional bonus
of Uncle Harry's elasticated armbands, the rest of the house
certainly made up for it.

It was built of red bricks, and had bay windows and a slate
roof. I imagine it was erected in late Victorian times, and was
solidly built.

There was a small front garden in which I vaguely remember London Pride growing in a narrow border. There was
also a thriving Pyracanthus shrub which climbed over the
front of the house, and had masses of scarlet berries in the
autumn. At my urgent request, Aunt Jess risked life and limb
during this season by hanging out of the bedroom window
with a pair of scissors, and cutting off branches for me, as I
waited below, so that I could take them to school to adorn
our classroom.

There was also a fascinating round metal lid in the front
path which the coal man could lift up. He shot his sacks of
coal down the chute here, and the thunderous rumbling mass
fell straight into the coal cellar which ran under the hall of the
house.

Access to this terrifying place was by means of a few steps
down from a door immediately outside the kitchen. An

enamel candlestick and a box of matches stood on a shelf just inside, and by this wavering light the cavern could be explored. There were recesses on the right-hand side which once held bottles of wine, no doubt, but I can't think that Grandma had many of those in store there.

From the front door, the hall seemed long to a child. My sister, when about six years old, used to wait in silent dread for the aunts to send her to the front door to collect the evening paper, which had been thrust through the letter-box.

She was convinced that the Kaiser himself, complete with waxed moustache and spiked helmet, was lurking behind the heavy curtains on the first landing. It was only a matter of time before he came thundering down the stairs to catch her before she regained the safety of the kitchen.

Grandma Read and the two aunts naturally had no idea of this nightly torture and when, years later, my sister confessed, they were stricken with remorse, poor dears.

The doors opened from the hall on the left. The first led into Grandma's drawing-room and the second into the dining-room directly behind it.

The drawing-room was a great favourite of mine – it had so many attractive things in it. The furniture was upholstered in red plush and there was a matching red carpet on the floor. Iridescent conch shells stood on the marble mantelpiece, and there was a fascinating bead fire screen which was attached by a brass contraption to the mantel shelf.

The screen was composed of tiny beads depicting arum

lilies on a green background of leaves. Two heavy gold tassels hung at each corner, and the whole thing seemed beautiful to me.

The piano was much used, as I have mentioned. It was an upright model, and some of Aunt Rose's handiwork, I suspect, appeared on its top in the form of a black satin runner embroidered with pink and red braid. Some of her pictures adorned the walls, and in brackets on each side of the over-mantel were tufts of dried blue statice.

A small octagonal table stood in the centre of the room, and this was inlaid with a pattern of ivy leaves. Another black satin mat, suitably embellished by Aunt Rose, stood in the middle of this table on which a potted fern was sometimes lodged.

Double doors behind the red plush sofa folded back to give access to the dining-room. This was done at Christmas time, or at weddings or other family occasions.

Above the double doors, flat against the wall, was a green glass walking-stick suspended there by two ribbons. I should like to have played with it, as well as the conch shells and some china cherubs which sported themselves on top of the piano (no nonsense here about having the lid open!) but I was not allowed to handle Grandma's treasures, at least not when her eye was upon me.

Years later, I described this room in a book called *The Market Square*, where a prosperous Caxley ironmonger called Bender North was to be found taking his ease, after the shop was closed below, in his splendid drawing-room.

A gas fire warmed this room and another heated the dining-room. Before each stood a small dish of water 'to purify the air', I was told.

The dining-room was rather dark and was furnished with a long mahogany table surrounded by heavily-built mahogany chairs upholstered in some shiny black material which was probably American cloth. In one corner was a rather handsome piece of furniture in which was kept the best glass and china. Its name appealed to me, and I liked to hear Grandma directing Aunt Jess to bring something from 'the shiffernear'. (I have just looked up 'chiffonier' in the *Oxford Dictionary* and see that it is described as 'a movable low cupboard with a sideboard top', but I don't think that Grandma's specimen could have been

moved very often as it was stuffed with heavy breakables.)

A conservatory opened out from the dining-room with a door from it into the garden. On family occasions, such as weddings, the children were settled in there at bamboo tables covered with starched linen cloths, at liberty to drop their crumbs on the tiled floor without being scolded. I remember we had fairy lights strung in there once. These were little glass jars, rather like fish-paste jars, in different colours and glowing from a small candle or night-light placed inside.

The first flight of stairs from the hall ended in two heavy dark curtains which had to be drawn aside on large brass rings to disclose a landing where Grandma's bedroom lay ahead, at the back of the house, over the kitchen and scullery, and the lavatory and bathroom stood on the left. It was behind these curtains that my quaking sister imagined that the Kaiser lay in wait for her.

The bath was encased in wood, and so was the wash basin in the corner with its brass taps above it. It was a rather dark room and the small window was either of frosted glass or covered with that patterned oiled paper, beloved of Victorians, which ensured complete privacy.

The lavatory next door was equally gloomy and I seemed to spend an inordinate amount of time there after breakfast at my aunts' urgent promptings to '*try*, dear'. However, it was a quiet peaceful place, and I swung my short legs and let my mind drift very happily, successfully ignoring the growing agitation of my two aunts as the clock's hands crept inexorably forward and my mission proved in vain. I can never remember Grandma Read getting in the least perturbed by all this fuss. After twelve children, she had become philosophical, no doubt, about such transient things.

Grandma Read's bedroom was probably the one best known to me as it was here that I was put for my afternoon rest in pre-school, or holiday times. Here I was divested of my pinafore, frock and shoes, and tucked up under the eiderdown in just my vest, liberty bodice, chemise, knickers (edged with cotton crochet work which left a delightful pattern on one's thighs) petticoat and socks.

It was usually Aunt Jess who performed this task and

before she departed downstairs I would plead with her to let me have a china ornament from the mantelpiece. It portrayed a little girl in a sprigged skirt accompanied by a dog, and I loved to take it to bed with me. As dear Aunt Jess was putty in my hands, I invariably won, and the pretty thing was given to me with many cautions about 'taking-great-care-not-to-drop-it-or-what-will-Grandma say?'

I knew better than to ask my Grandma for it on the rare occasions when she put me to rest. She would give me her wonderful smile, a quick kiss, a brisk, 'No!' and that would be that.

As soon as Aunt Jess had gone, I got out of bed, china ornament in hand, and explored the room. Grandma's dressing-table, complete with seven or eight little lace mats and a runner, called collectively a duchesse set, had such

entrancing things as scent bottles, hair brushes, combs, powder jars and so on which I investigated thoroughly. There was also a cone-like object hanging by a ribbon from the mirror's knob, called a hair tidy. It was the same shape as the paper cone which the grocer whipped up from a flat piece of thick blue paper on the counter ready for filling with sugar from a scoop.

I usually examined the contents of the small drawers during rest time. The larger ones were too heavy to pull out. The little drawers held trinkets, small hair combs, little pots of face cream, nail scissors and the like.

I enjoyed combing my own hair and then the fringe of Grandma's hearth rug with her largest comb, and was sorely tempted to undo the end of the pink or blue stitching which bound Grandma's blankets. If you worked hard, it was possible to make a dear little ball of pink or blue wool when it had all unravelled, but my mother had not been pleased when my sister and I presented her with the fruits of our labours, and I never risked it with Grandma's blankets, much as I should have enjoyed this innocent pastime.

The bedroom window looked out over the back garden. There was nothing much of excitement in it, although at one stage Aunt Rose kept some hens there and, one afternoon, a resourceful young cousin, aged two, successfully painted the run and the less-agile chickens pale blue.

The garden next door, however, was a miracle of neatness, small clipped box hedges surrounding the garden beds. Here Eileen lived, a most beautiful child and to me 'a big girl' of about seven. She was as immaculate as the garden, dressed in white, with fair ringlets and a stunning dolls' pram which she

pushed happily round and round the paths. Her white buckskin boots never appeared soiled, her clothes were unsullied, she had a charming smile and pretty manners. If Eileen were there to look at, during my rest hour, my happiness was complete, and I would watch her as I sucked the china girl's head and hope that she would look up and wave to me.

The top half of Grandma's door to the landing was made of glass, and in each corner was a pane of coloured glass with an engraved star in the middle.

The top two, of course, were beyond my reach, but one ruby red pane and one dark blue in the bottom half afforded me infinite pleasure. How enthralling to see the landing wardrobe and, if the curtains were pulled back, the whole of the first flight of stairs, the hall stand and the front door, glowing redly as if about to burst into flames! Equally enjoyable, with one eye pressed to the blue pane, was the same view plunged into mysterious gloom. Often when busily experimenting with these sublime colours, Aunt Jess would appear at the foot of the stairs, red as the winter sun, or murky as an underwater mermaid, and I knew it was time to fly back to bed and pull up the eiderdown.

'Had a nice rest, darling?' she would say.

I always had.

The next floor comprised Uncle Harry's little room, a fair-sized landing, and the main bedroom, over the drawing-room, which Aunt Rose and Aunt Jess shared.

There was a large bay window from which Aunt Jess hung to cut the Pyracanthus branches for me. The walls were pink and the paintwork of a light colour, but to me the chief attraction was the gas burner which swivelled out from the wall on a brass bracket.

When lit, the flame was shaped like a fish tail, blue in the middle and flaring yellow at the edges. Aunt Jess heated her hair tongs in this and curled her fringe and various stray ends, to the accompaniment of much blue smoke and a strong smell of singeing.

The bay window looked across Hither Green Lane to the trees which surrounded a hospital, known as the Fever Hospital. I don't think I ever saw the building itself, but its trees were very pleasant to look upon over the wooden fence. The room always seemed to get a good deal of sunshine, and was probably the lightest room in that rather dark house.

Up the last flight of stairs lay Aunt Jess's workroom and, above Grandma's, a nice square bedroom which looked out over the garden.

This was the spare room, and always seemed to be in use either by older cousins, a visiting married aunt, or simply by the overflow of Aunt Jess's work which might be spread out, ready tacked for someone's fitting, either on the white counterpane or draped over the brass bedrail.

I believe there were attics above these two rooms, for I vaguely remember a trap door in the ceiling at the head of these stairs, but I was never lucky enough to explore beyond these limits. In any case, by the time one had pounded up all those stairs behind Aunt Jess, three-year-old legs were quite tired enough.

Sometimes I could persuade Aunt Jess to co-operate with me in delightful game with the bells which still operated in every room in the house. These had a white china handle and were fixed beside the various fireplaces. By giving them a half-turn, a pleasant jangling sound could be heard in the distance. A box hung outside the kitchen door, near the door to the cellar, and here the bells rang cheerfully and indicated which room needed attention. I preferred ringing the bells, rushing from room to room, but if Aunt Jess could be prevailed upon to do this, which was not often, I was very content to study the result outside the kitchen door.

Altogether it was a fascinating house for a young child to explore, but its chief attraction, I now see as I look back, was the affection with which my sister and I were surrounded. Grandma Read, Aunt Rose, Aunt Jess and Uncle Harry were all busy people, but each of them could spare time and love for us.

A SAD ENDING

WHEN the war was over my mother, never very strong, had to undergo surgery.

In 1921, we moved farther out into the country so that she would be in the healthy surroundings of the North Downs. It was a summer of extreme heat and drought, and the position of our new home on the heights gave no hint in those first glorious months of the sort of bitter cold which could be expected during the many winters we lived there.

However, my mother rallied well and began to enjoy country pursuits such as gardening, cycling and taking an active part in the local Women's Institute and the Glee Club, and later the church choir. Both she and my father sang well.

Naturally, Grandma Read, the aunts and Uncle Harry were frequent visitors. My father revelled in this new-found freedom after four years of active service and the anxiety of my mother's illness, and enjoyed entertaining.

The aunts were enthusiastic about the new home. I don't think Uncle Harry really took it in at all, but Grandma Read was not much impressed. As a Londoner, she much preferred a landscape with figures, and on looking at the spectacular views which our windows commanded over some miles of rolling Kentish fields and woods, she shook her head sadly.

'It's all much *too green*!' she told my father, who relished the remark to the end of his days.

Grandma Read must have been around seventy-five when we moved away. She was still spry, still fond of her weekly trips to the cinema, and still blessed with beautiful dark hair.

She had enjoyed good health throughout her life, despite the large family she had borne, and she dreaded 'becoming a burden to anyone', as she put it.

Her father had lived with her until he died well on in his nineties, and perhaps the remembrance of all that had needed to be done for him accentuated her horror of being dependent upon her own children.

It was a year or so after our move that she died. I had returned from a meeting of the local Brownies one hot evening, and was surprised to see my mother looking red-eyed and tremulous.

She broke the news of Grandma's death to me, as I demolished a late tea, and although I felt vaguely sad at the thought of not seeing her again, it seemed to me that anyone as old as Grandma Read could not be expected to live much longer. My mother's grief seemed to be unnecessarily severe in the circumstances.

It was some time afterwards that I learnt that Grandma Read, after a day or two's slight indisposition, had decided that she might after all become the burden she so feared to be, and ended her life at the age of seventy-six, by taking poison.

Grandma Shafe

Alice Shafe (neé Batt)
1860–1933

GRANDMA SHAFE

MY FATHER'S mother was a complete contrast in looks to Grandma Read. She was considerably taller, was fair-skinned and had a mass of fluffy white curls. She was also very large. Grandma Read probably weighed about seven stone. My guess is that Grandma Shafe probably tipped the scales at over twelve.

She dressed well, and always looked beautifully turned out despite her bulk. I don't think that I ever saw her undressed, but her corsets must have been formidable.

She favoured lighter colours than Grandma Read, and wore mainly blues, greys and purples. She had a number of toques, many with veiling over the face, and these sometimes matched the loose coats which reached her calves or ankles. The fashions beloved of the late Queen Mary, who was seven years younger, were those which my Grandma Shafe followed, and which suited her very well.

She was a jolly person with round merry eyes of grey, and a wheezy laugh which was a good deal in evidence. She was particularly fond of my father, with whom she had much in common, and he was always able to amuse her to the point of reducing her to tears of delight as she fought for breath through her laughter.

It was a very good thing that she had a sense of humour for my Grandfather had very little and had been a repressive father, but I will say more of Thomas Smith Shafe later. Many years afterwards, when she was living with her daughter Eva, Grandma Shafe was asked why on earth she had married him. The answer was poignant.

'Well, dear, you see, I wasn't very happy at home.'

Surely this might stand as an epitaph to many unhappy marriages made when girls looked upon their weddings as the main aim in life.

Nevertheless, she was a loyal and hard-working wife to the man of her choice, and her children adored her.

She had been born Alice Batt, in 1860, I think in London, but I know little about her parents. Certainly she had admirers, and with her gaiety and cheerful disposition this was to be expected. One suitor she would have married, she said later, but her parents strongly disapproved and she obeyed them.

When, or how, she met Thomas Shafe I do not know for sure, but suspect that it was probably through the church. He was a good-looking young man, fair-haired and blue-eyed, very straight and slim. His looks probably attracted her, and his serious nature probably appealed to her parents who, no doubt, were anxious to see their lively and attractive daughter settled with a responsible man. It is possible that she still secretly mourned the young man whom she had refused, but certainly she was still young, only twenty-one, when she married Thomas Smith Shafe on Christmas Day in 1881.

They set up house in a respectable suburb in east London, possibly in Manor Park or Leytonstone where there was a good public transport service to central London.

Thomas was employed in a fairly responsible position at the Post Office in Mount Pleasant, and travelled daily to his clerical work.

They always rented houses until retirement when they bought 17 New Pier Street at Walton-on-the-Naze in Essex, where I first remember them. Evidently, rented property suited them very well and they had plenty of choice in those days. It was the habit of my grandfather to move somewhere in the

eastern suburbs every three or four years when he felt that his present abode needed redecoration. The mind boggles at the thought of so many domestic upheavals, but evidently Grandma accepted them with her customary good humour.

Thomas suffered severely from claustrophobia, as later my father did, and his family had chosen Walton-on-the-Naze as a suitable holiday centre when he and his brother and sisters were young, because there were no tunnels to negotiate from Liverpool Street Station.

Consequently, young Tom was fond of this little seaside resort, and it is not surprising that he kept up his visits to it and finally retired there in the early months of 1914.

SUMMER 1914

O UR first visit to the new home must have been in that fateful summer. My sister was then four years old, and I was fifteen months. It was during this stay at Walton that the frontispiece photograph of us was taken.

My sister is doing all that she has been told to do by the photographer. She has her legs crossed at the ankle, one hand supporting me, and a polite smile in evidence.

On the contrary, I am being obstinate, but it is the photographer's fault entirely as he has been trying to wrest my adored teddy from me on the grounds that he is too shabby to be recorded for posterity. What utter snobbery! As you see, I am having no truck with such a despicable fellow, and refuse to cross my legs at the ankle – even if I could with that figure – or smile. And teddy remains firmly in my grip.

Our clothes are worth noticing. We are wearing identical outfits of warm skirts and woollen high-necked jerseys, and very suitable summer wear too for playing on an east-coast beach with the icy North Sea pounding a few yards away. We got to know those splendid stretches of firm sand very well, but I can never remember finding them too hot.

My father was an Army reservist, and so was called up at the outbreak of war, on August 4th, to the Royal Horse Artillery. His twenty-seventh birthday was two days later, and he was in France very soon after that.

I do not remember visiting my grandparents' new home whilst he was away at what was confusingly called 'The Front'. (There seemed to be two fronts. One overseas where my father was busy with guns and horses, and the other between our house and the gate into the road, where the path was tiled and London Pride and privet grew.)

But later in the war years, either late 1917 or early 1918, my father came home – mercifully unharmed – and was posted to St John's Wood where he was an army riding instructor.

He took us, as small children, to see the stables and the horses he adored, and I was put on the back of one of those noble beasts. I screamed blue murder until I was rescued. My

father, I feel sure, was more concerned about the horse's reaction to such a ghastly noise than about my fears, but I am thankful to say that I have never had to sit on a horse since that day.

No doubt we visited my grandparents during that period, and certainly after the war it was our annual holiday place, and my main recollections of Grandma Shafe really begin when I was about six or seven years of age.

Unlike my Grandma Read who had a long family of twelve children, of which my mother was number eleven, Grandma Shafe had only four as far as I know, and I heard of no sad infant deaths which were such a common feature then of family life.

The first was a boy, named Frederick. He left home in his teens and eventually went to America where he married and had a son, called June – or so it is recorded in the family tree. Could he *really* be June? Or might he be Juan? Who knows? Anyway, with a Harlene on the maternal side of the family, it might well be June.

Frederick did not appear again. He and Grandpa had parted on frosty terms, I gather.

My father was christened Arthur Gunnis Shafe and was the second son, born in 1887. Grandpa Shafe, who was longing for a daughter, was not very pleased, but evidently my father was a model baby and, judging by a photograph of him sitting up in a go-cart about the age of eighteen months, in a very fetching white bonnet with a huge crown and a satin bow under the chin, he was a fine boy, and already using the

winning smile which made him so many friends when he was older.

A year or two later, Grandma Shafe was again expecting a baby, and this time she sincerely hoped it would be a girl for Tom's sake.

It was not. George Herbert Shafe duly appeared, and Grandpa was so disgusted that he refused to go upstairs to see the new baby. Poor Grandma! This little unwanted one grew up to be one of our favourite uncles.

At last, in 1891, Grandma produced the longed-for daughter who was christened Eva. She was a beautiful child with the clear blue eyes of her father, and she grew into one of the handsomest women I ever met. She inherited her mother's energy and gaiety, was athletic, generous and warm-hearted. It was Eva who took on the main responsibility of looking after her parents in the last years of their lives, and lived up to Thomas's ideal of the perfect daughter he had always wanted.

There were no more children. Perhaps Grandma Shafe decided that to risk another son might be carrying things too far. Four children were quite enough responsibility.

GRANDPA SHAFE

PERHAPS this is the moment to have a short account of Thomas Shafe's family.

His father was William James Shafe who was born in 1827 and who married in 1851 a girl called Emma Eliza Gunnis. My father's second name was Gunnis after his grandmother's maiden name.

William and Emma had four children. A daughter, named Emma Lydia, then my grandfather Thomas. Another daughter, Ada, followed in 1858 and the youngest child, called Edward James, was born in 1861.

I was not destined to meet my great-aunts and great-uncles although they all lived to a ripe old age. The exception was Edward whom I met when he was an elderly man approaching seventy, and the circumstances were most unusual. But more of that later.

We did not meet them for the simple reason that Thomas had left home as soon as he could, and would have nothing to do with his family. Mind you, we only knew one side of the story, and the family may well have asked him to depart.

He was always a difficult man, and I suspect that he had been a sore trial to his sisters and brother. He was quite sure that he was always right, was narrow-mindedly religious, relishing the taboos imposed by Victorian standards so that, as children, we were never allowed to play on the beach or read anything other than the prescribed holy books allowed by Grandpa on a Sunday.

'Remember the Sabbath Day to keep it holy' was a rule he tried to live by, and very trying it was to the rest of the household. I can't remember that cooking a substantial midday Sunday dinner came within this rule. Maybe, women's work was exempt.

His sons used to point out that he should not read the Monday edition of a newspaper as men had certainly been employed in producing it on the Sabbath but, like so many obstinate people, Grandpa was able to bend the rules to suit himself.

Smoking he abhorred, and I expect he had been censorious about this as a youth. My great-uncle Edward enjoyed a cigar in his later years, I recall. No doubt brother Tom had pointed out that the downward path to hell awaited him as a smoker.

A copy of the New Testament presented to me when I was about eight
years of age had a note in Grandpa's
hand in the margin against the passage:

'And he that is filthy, let him be
filthy still.'

'*i. e. Tobacco smokers*' wrote my grandfather.

There were other remarks of a like nature, aimed at enlighten-
ing the young mind, but that is the one which I most clearly
remember.

He had also scored across the pages showing St Paul's
journeys. The first journey had one line, the second two, and
the third had three lines, almost beautifully ruled using a fine
J nib. I think he enjoyed teaching.

His mind was clear, his diction precise, and he was fond of
his grandchildren so long as they were completely obedient
and quiet. But there was nothing warm and happy about
him, and the strict rules of behaviour which he imposed
upon himself – and tried to impose, unsuccessfully as it
turned out, upon his family – gave him a wintry rectitude
and a 'holier-than-thou' attitude which made him very few
friends.

He was a lay preacher and spent a great deal of time in
his study writing his discourses. There were hundreds of
books – *Spurgeon's Sermons* figured prominently – but to
my infant eyes there was not a readable one among the lot.

Not that we were encouraged to go into the study. Grandpa
used it as his sanctum, and probably dozed in there as often as
he studied.

This lay-preaching was not something which he had
taken up on retirement. Evidently he had been interested

in such things from early times, and my
father used to enact a vivid imitation of
Grandpa rapping on his study window,
peering over the top of his spectacles,
and calling out to his young sons in the
garden, 'Go away, you boys! Go away!'
when the ball had bounced against the
window and disturbed his train of
thought.

Sundays must have been particularly
irksome to his young family. Years
later, when my sister and I used to
stay there alone as children, the heavy hand of sabbatical
stricture was still in evidence.

In a drawer of his desk in the study, he kept about half a
dozen paper-backed stories which he considered suitable reading for a young child on a Sunday afternoon.

Older people may remember some of these lugubrious
effusions. The titles of those I remember were *Froggy's Little
Brother, Buy Your Own Cherries* and *Christie's Old Organ*, and
they dealt with sanctimonious children, usually dying of some
lingering disease, who engaged in very unchildlike pursuits
such as saving drunken fathers or reuniting parted parents. All
were written in mawkish prose, revolting to any normal
child, and simply asking to be parodied.

Luckily, my grandfather always retired again into his
study after presenting us with our reading matter, and im-
pressing upon us the need to keep it clean. He probably had
a nap.

Grandma, as soon as the door was shut, relieved us of these
dreadful books and substituted such welcome alternatives as a
pile of *Home Chat*, a cheerful women's magazine, in which
we followed the adventures of a dear little black boy called

Epaminondas with considerable relish. It occurs to me that such stories would now be banned as 'racist'. All I can say is that Epaminondas did more to encourage a happy relationship between black and white children than any Race Relations Board could do.

Of course, if our parents were with us, we were spared the horrors of Grandpa's Sunday observances, and spent the day out of the house, either on the beach or in the shelter of Grandpa's beach hut.

When I think of Grandpa Shafe now, I see him, thin, clean-shaven with very blue eyes, and dressed in his every-day retirement attire of a fine grey woollen roll-neck pullover and grey flannels to match.

He liked to stand with his back to the fire, warming his bony hands behind him. Those fingers were devastatingly strong when it came to tickling his grandchildren's ribs which he sometimes did when in an indulgent mood.

He was always spruce and immaculately clean and I think he loved us in his bleak way.

THE BEACH HUT

THE beach hut was a source of great pleasure to us. Originally, it had been sited half way down the cliff beside the steps which led to the beach.

The cliffs in that part of the east coast were much given to erosion. I can remember the terror which gripped me when I saw a garden on the cliff top gradually being eaten away, plants and shrubs sliding topsy-turvy down the incline. Eventually, the house itself went the same way, but luckily the people who lived in it had moved somewhere safer well before the fateful night.

After a few minor landslides it was deemed prudent to shift the beach hut, and Grandpa was lucky in securing a much better site directly on the promenade, so that we could run straight across the pavement to the lovely hard sand. This meant that we did not have to negotiate the stairs nor the muddy cliff path, all of which must have resulted in a much cleaner beach hut.

The floor was always slightly gritty from our sandy plimsolls, and there was a marvellous salty smell compounded of natural ozone and the creosote with which the exterior was painted once a year.

A long cushioned bench stood against the wall, and there were a number of deck chairs and a folding table. On the wall was a cupboard containing such useful things as a tea tin, sugar jar, cups and sauces and cutlery. There was a First-Aid tin, too.

There were also some cards with which we played Snap and Beggar-Your-Neighbour, and board games of Snakes and Ladders, Ludo and so on. I expect there were Draughts too, as Grandpa was a dab hand at this game, and thoroughly enjoyed huffing his way to swift victory.

Here we changed into our bathing clothes and emerged, shivering, to make the long walk to the sea. Unless the tide were really high, splashing exuberantly about the breakwaters, bathing at Walton meant a long trek through knee-high waves until one could submerge. My parents and grandparents considered it much safer at this stage and, blue with the cold, my sister and I obediently splashed out into the North Sea.

Sometimes we paddled instead, and this I much preferred. For one thing, we kept on our comfortable warm clothes, simply stuffing our skirts into garments called our 'paddling drawers'.

Our paddling drawers were made of sponge-cloth with pink and grey stripes, *round* us, of course. We must have looked like spinning tops. Some of our youthful fellow-paddlers had drawers made of mackintosh, which must have been far more effective.

However, we were quite happy with our own garments. What did aggrieve us was the fact that we were not allowed to have metal spades.

'So easy to cut off your toes, my dear, with those horrid sharp things,' said Grandma.

And so we were obliged to struggle on with our sissy wooden tools whilst children half our age were slicing through the lovely crisp sand, and knocking up enormous castles in much less time.

We played cricket and tennis on those vast stretches of sandy beach, marking out the lines with our despised spades. We also played a simpler game called French Cricket which involved shielding one's legs with a tennis racket while others tried to hit them with a soft ball. The worst moments were when the attackers had closed in, and there you were, racket in trembling hand, knees knocking, whilst the hot breath of the enemy blew the sand from one's legs.

Then it was back to the shelter of the beach hut, to the kettle humming on the spirit stove and lovely sticky buns. There we would be out of the cruel wind which always seemed to blow, however halcyon the weather, straight from Russia.

AN OUTING WITH GRANDMA

M Y GRANDFATHER owned a plot of land between Walton-on-the-Naze and Frinton-on-Sea. This plot also had a hut on it, and occasionally in the summer we went for a picnic there.

My grandmother, whose bulk was impressive, could not walk a great distance, and sometimes a carriage was hired to take her to this picnic spot. I was lucky enough to accompany her one hot afternoon in the carriage which I think was called a landau, but I am not very well up in carriage lore. In any case, it was an open affair with seating comfortably for four people, and a little flight of steps which folded up, or were let down to allow easy entry.

The seats were of leather and deliciously hot against bare thighs. No doubt I was wearing white socks and white cotton drawers edged with crochet made by Grandma herself. The crochet work was the size and shape of joined-up butter beans and left a red pattern on the back of one's thighs.

The driver sat high on a box in front, and held the reins in one hand and a whip in the other – not that it was ever used. The horse ambled along, while Grandma nodded her veiled toque or lifted a gloved hand to friends as we passed.

She had with her a grey parasol of watered silk. At the end of the malacca handle was a round pink china knob, and on it

was a minute scene of an unknown pier and seascape. At our feet was a basket with our picnic tea, and over all lay a snowy linen tea cloth.

The carriage stopped at the side of the road, only a few yards' walk across the field which belonged to Grandpa. Strangely enough, I remember nothing of the hut or the picnic or even of the return journey. But what is unforgettable is that short walk through the field on the edge of the cliff.

The sun blazed down upon a sea of scarlet poppies giving out their hot peppery scent from the crumpled papery petals. Lark song spilled from a vivid blue sky above – a sky that merged imperceptibly with the distant blue sea. The air was strong and heady. The grass, brittle and warm, soon clouded my best shoes with dust.

Grandma had put up her parasol. Behind us, the driver carried the picnic basket. Holding my hot hand in her own gloved one, we picked our way through the poppies to the delights which now I have forgotten.

Later, I believe, Grandpa's plot suffered the fate of so many cliff-top properties and slid into the hungry sea one wild night of storm, taking with it the hut, the poppies, the larks' nests and many memories.

GOING TO GRANDMA'S

THE journey to visit our grandparents at Walton was quite an adventure.

Later, when we were the proud owners of a Ford car, complete with canvas hood and side curtains, we drove from London through Chelmsford and Colchester and arrived in time for tea. But, in the early days, we either went by train or by steamer.

I much preferred the latter, as Liverpool Street Station was my idea of hell. The noise and filth from the steam trains terrified and upset me. We used to cross a horrifying iron bridge under the grimy glass roof of the station. Below, the trains snorted and puffed out steam and smoke which eddied round one's legs, or sometimes hid one's parents from sight, causing agonising panic. Now and again, an ear-splitting scream came from the engines, and men with black faces peered from their sides. They held shovels very often, and the red glare from the fire box heightened the satanic effect.

Once we were safely inside the railway compartment, things became a little less fraught. Our cases were put on the rack, including my favourite made of plaited straw and secured with a strap round it.

It was interesting to see the little gardens of the East End trundling by. Some had washing all a-blow, some held a poor dog on a chain, or hutches with captive rabbits. Sometimes a lucky free cat squatted four-square on a wall or on the top of a coal bin, and sometimes small children waved to the train.

Later, as the suburbs were left behind, the flat fields of Essex spread away to the coast line.

'A penny for the one who sees the sea first!' my father would say.

And somewhere near Frinton, sure enough, the sea could be glimpsed and the penny won.

Once out of the train, the salt sea air engulfed us. We breathed it in in great gulps.

There was Grandpa, bending for a kiss. Grandma was at home, preparing a welcoming tea. My sister and I ran ahead, down the slope to New Pier Street, while behind us the grown-ups talked of such dull things as their health, the journey and the weather.

*

It was far better to go to Walton by sea. In those days the *Belle* Steamers used to start from Tower Bridge. There were several of these magnificent paddle steamers. There was the *Brighton Belle*, and the *Clacton Belle* and the *Southend Belle*. There may have been more *Belles*, but they are the only ones I can recall. Later, I believe, there was the *Royal Sovereign*.

They set off from Tower Bridge at eight o'clock in the morning, so that we had to make an early start whether we set off from Lewisham, or later from Chelsfield.

We travelled on the old London, South Eastern and Chatham Railway. On each side of the door was a small brass plate, like a miniature nutmeg scraper, for the use of smokers who ignited their matches on them. A heavy leather strap let down or pulled up the window, and across the bottom of the window frame ran the warning in two languages.

Do not lean out of the window
Ne pas se pencher dehors

The latter, of course, was for the poor French travellers, making for Charing Cross, who might be ignorant of the superior tongue and possibly quite used to putting their heads out of French trains.

We passed through all the familiar stations, Orpington, Chislehurst, Hither Green, New Cross and so on, with the exception of Petts Wood which, in those days, was a somewhat marshy tract with no identifying landmarks. We watched it turn from undistinguished fields to a spreading suburb over the years.

It was at London Bridge, if I remember rightly, that we got out.

Somehow, I connect Billingsgate with our approach to Tower Bridge, but it might well have been on another outing that I marvelled at the fish porters balancing towers of fish-boxes on their hard flat hats, with ribbons of grey slime dangling unheeded on each side of their red faces.

The steamer had wooden slatted seats on deck, and here we spent most of our time, though hanging over the railings watching the river water, and then the real sea, churning away beneath us was equally enthralling. There was a snug little cabin affair where one could get hot drinks, but it was advisable to give the lavatories a miss, if humanly possible, as inevitably some poor wretch would be there feeling sea-sick.

My father, who loved every minute on the steamer, insisted on taking us below to see the engines which fascinated him. As a very young man, he had spent some time training in Yarrow's, the marine engineers, who then had a shipyard on the Thames, somewhere near Greenwich, I believe. Here he met another young fellow, Chris Read, who took him home where he was introduced to Chris's sister Grace, who later became our mother.

Father's eyes sparkled as he helped us down and ushered us along gangways between pulsing pistons, turning wheels and great thumping lumps of metal, gleaming with greeny-gold oil and smelling revolting. I think that Father would have stayed there for the whole journey if he had been alone, but family duties took him back to the deck eventually, much to our relief.

I suppose we sometimes called at Southend Pier, which was a very long one, but it always seemed to be stranded in miles of glistening grey mud as we churned round the Thames Estuary and made northward, for the next stop, Clacton.

We had a picnic on deck and cups of tea from the little refreshment cabin to warm us up. Our faces glowed from the salt winds, and our hair was in stringy tangles which were going to be agony to comb through when we arrived.

Walton Pier was reached in the afternoon. There was a tremendous racket of engines as the ship edged towards the end of the pier, and much shouting and throwing of enormous greasy hawsers. Then the great paddle steamer nudged its way against the landing stage and the pier shuddered with the impact. Gangways were heaved into place, and unsteadily we disembarked.

Grandpa would be waiting for us, and we then mounted the pier tram and had the final exhilarating part of the long journey. It was marvellous to trundle over the heaving waves far below for over a mile and then to gain the well-known buildings on the esplanade, the turnstile, the automatic machines, and the nostalgic smell of weather-boarding, rusting cast-iron and salt spray mingled together to make a Walton welcome.

Our excitement at arriving at Grandma's back door was slightly quelled by Father reminding us to wipe our perfectly clean shoes on the door-scraper by the step.

It made us realize that, no matter how warm was Grandma's hug, nor how splendid the tea spread in readiness, it was here that we had to mind our manners, and to be extremely careful not to annoy our grandfather.

We knew of old, and had been reminded several times before our arrival, that the freedom we enjoyed at home and at Grandma Read's was somewhat restricted at 17 New Pier Street. This we accepted. It was all part and parcel of a holiday at Grandma's, and we learnt to respect the conditions which were there imposed.

17 New Pier Street

OUR first visit on arriving was to Grandma's bathroom which was upstairs.

I can still remember the lovely smell of Grandma's Erasmic Violet soap, its oval shape and beautiful purple colour, with which we washed our hands – filthy from the steamer and the tram.

Grandpa's soap was on the wooden bath rack which spanned the white bath. His, as befitted such an ascetic character, was plain Lifebuoy, and its fresh carbolic smell mingled with Grandma's Erasmic to give an unforgettable fragrance.

Next door to the bathroom was the bedroom which my sister and I shared while we were there. It was a square, sunny room over the kitchen, and looked out upon the small neat garden. Its great attraction for us was the pair of Staffordshire china dogs which stood one at each end of the mantelpiece.

The double bed was covered with a white honeycomb bedspread which I believe was called a marcella counterpane. They were in much favour at this time, had a fringe at each side and were easily washed.

Our father and mother were housed along the corridor in a bedroom which lay over my grandfather's study. It was not as brilliantly light as our own for the one window was partially shaded by the side of the house.

The third bedroom was at the front of the building and was considerably larger. Here my grandparents slept, and I remember little about its furnishings except that the general impact was of large pieces of well-polished mahogany, and curtains discreetly drawn two-thirds of the way across the windows.

Below this room was the drawing-cum-dining room, dominated by a large oil painting of a Victorian gentleman in dark clothes. I never knew who he was, but his eyes followed one wherever one stood in the room, which was a little disconcerting. Perhaps he was a Shafe, or Batt, or even a Gunnis. No doubt he ended up in a saleroom, and the handsome gold frame alone should have brought in something.

The windows looked out upon the quiet side street, and Grandma frequently sat here watching the neighbours go by as she did her crocheting.

Under the stairs stood an armchair, the sort with a carpet seat and painted wooden arms which would fold up. Upon this stood the pile of women's magazines beloved by Grandma, and among them the *Home Chats* which would provide us with mental refreshment on Sunday afternoons.

Almost opposite the chair was the door to Grandpa's study. Normally, I imagine, it would have been the household's dining-room, but here it was the place, as I

have explained earlier, where Grandpa retired to write or read his theological articles, or simply took refuge from the mundane world of cooking, cleaning and the chatter of Grandma's friends.

The kitchen, which led directly into the little garden, was the real heart of the house, and had that vivid seaside luminosity which came from the great East Anglian sky.

Here Grandma cooked her splendid meals, succulent roasts, shiny brown pies, gooseberry tarts and bursting sausages.

My sister and I squeezed together on a small window-seat, my father and mother sat at each end, and Grandpa and Grandma sat in their usual places in front of the gleaming kitchen range.

My grandfather always said grace, which we had to remember, as it was unforgivable to pick up knife and fork before this little ceremony. We also had grace at the end of a meal, and I can still remember the time when my grandfather, knees bent and eyes shut, said grace whilst holding a milk jug in one hand and a plate of cake in the other.

We had had tea in the garden, sitting on the white slatted seat there, and he had begun to clear the table when he remembered that grace had not been said.

'We thank Thee O Lord for this Thy bounty. Amen.'

We echoed the Amen. Grandpa's knees straightened, he opened his eyes, and bore the food towards the kitchen.

He was an abstemious man, never drinking anything alcoholic, of course, and occasionally singing abstainers' songs, such as:

> I like to take a social glass
> But only when it is filled with WATER
> It makes the hours so pleasantly pass
> And fills the air with laughter.

I need hardly add that this filled my irreverent father with mirth, which he was prudent enough to suppress in his father's presence. Evidently, as boys, they were given little tracts showing the evil results of strong drink. I never had the luck to see one of these, but I gather that you started in the middle with a picture showing two men. One took to drink, and he proceeded from 'The social glass' (*not* filled with water), and then to reeling home where he beat his wife and children and went later, of course, to the pawnshop where he sold all his household goods for more drink. His family ended up, ragged and thin, outside the workhouse door, and he lay in the gutter in a dreadful stupor, or else in a pauper's coffin.

The other man's family was well-dressed and in blooming health, as all its members had in their glasses was what one of my uncles called 'Corporation Pop'. This man had a large house and garden, and a bank account to match. I must say, those Victorians had the knack of putting across a message, and I only wish I could have studied it first-hand.

Grandpa Shafe also ate very sparingly, and never left anything on his plate. He polished it with a piece of dry bread until any remnants of his first course had vanished. He then turned his plate over and was ready for a slice of apple tart, or a little cheese with a dry biscuit. What happened when the pudding course was stewed fruit and custard or a sloshy sort of trifle, I can't think, but I imagine that Grandma prevailed upon him to have another plate on those occasions.

It was a very pleasant house, and I think they had chosen well for their retirement. Not only was it in Grandpa's beloved Walton and near the beach, but it was a compact well-built house which Grandma could run easily. It was amazingly light. The woodwork and walls were lighter than in my Grandma Read's house, and the curtains were less heavy.

Looking back, and comparing the two, it seems to me that the house in Hither Green Lane was a Victorian one, and furnished in Victorian style, sombre and heavy. Grandma Shafe, some fourteen years younger than Grandma Read, was still comparatively young when Edward VII came to the throne and perhaps some of the gaiety of that era was reflected in the furnishings which appealed to her, and which she enjoyed buying when the time came for retirement in 1914.

In any case, the very atmosphere surrounding the two houses was startlingly different. The air of London was thick with the smoke of thousands of domestic, as well as industrial, chimneys. At Walton-on-the-Naze that air was clear and fresh, and sunlight was reflected from the vast sea and sands which bounded it.

No wonder we returned from our holidays in high spirits.

HOLIDAY RITUALS

THERE were certain rituals, rather like the 'Penny-for-the-one-who-sees-the-sea-first', connected with Walton.

One thing which we always did was to get up very early and accompany Father for a bracing pre-breakfast walk along the esplanade. On our way back we visited the baker's where we purchased enough hot rolls for the household's breakfast. There was a wonderful smell of fresh bread which added to the ravenous appetite already engendered by the early morning ozone.

Then there was the trip to Stone Point. This was undertaken in a rowing boat, nobly propelled by our father while Mother sat with the steering ropes over her shoulders and confused left with right. We trailed our hands, or our scorned wooden spades, helping the progress of the boat.

A picnic basket lay in the bottom, and there was always a melon for dessert. It would have been unthinkable to go to Stone Point without a melon on board.

Stone Point itself was a somewhat bleak stretch of fine sand loosely bound with marram grass. But the beach where we landed was of soft squelchy sand in which one sank up to one's knees when jumping from the boat. It was most frightening when we were really small but, as the years passed, we became quite blasé about it, and enjoyed tearing along this sea edge holding Father's hand, and roaring with laughter at the sucking sounds, the tumbles and the general exhilaration of all this exercise.

We had to keep a sharp eye open for the tide. It ebbed very quickly from this particular creek, and one terrifying occasion the rowing boat was caught in the mud and we began to fear that we should never return to the haven of Grandma's house. The mud smelt appalling, and there were grey and black clouds piling up at sea. I rather think some more holidaymakers came to our rescue, and helped to rock and tug at our boat until we were freed. It was wonderful to get back to New Pier Street after such an adventure, and this time we wiped our shoes thankfully on the door-scraper.

★ ★ ★

Of course there were other ways of going to Stone Point or the other places of interest on the Essex coast. One was by a public boat, much larger, called the *Minoru*.

These excursions were announced by the Walton Town Crier, who added considerably to the pleasure of our holidays. We would hear his hand-bell ringing while we were eating the hot rolls at breakfast. We all paused, cups suspended in mid-air, rolls half-way to mouths, to listen to his booming voice:

Oyez, oyez, oyez!
This is to give notice!
The *Minoru* will make a trip,
Down the river,
Leaving the Old Water Mill
At Ten Thirty
FARES ONE AND SIX!

Then he would announce other items of interest, more excursions, articles lost and found, and generally get the attention of all his listeners.

I wonder if there is still a Town Crier in that delectable little town.

LONG-LOST RELATIVES

O NE DAY when we were sitting in the beach hut, my father went for a stroll along the promenade and met a man and his wife who spoke to him.

They were accompanied by two small boys, one about six, the other just a toddler. The man introduced himself as Albert Shafe and said that he believed that the families were related.

It seemed miraculous to us as children that we should have stumbled across these relations. In fact, it was not really so surprising.

My grandfather and his brother Edward, my great-uncle Ted, had been taken to Walton-on-the-Naze as children, so it was natural that the place was known to his family, although Uncle Ted actually preferred to take his own children to such places as Herne Bay and Margate. He may not have wished, of course, to bump into brother Tom, who went there frequently and later, of course, lived there.

My father and this newly-found relative, Albert Shafe, the son of Edward Shafe, were first cousins, and had plenty to talk about. We soon made friends with the little boys, and the upshot was that they were all invited to visit us at Chelsfield. They so liked that area of Kent that later they bought a house quite near us, and we enjoyed their company for many years.

Uncle Albert had a magnificent voice and he and my father enjoyed singing together. This discovery of another branch of the family was of particular satisfaction to my father who was glad to feel that the breach between his father Tom and brother Ted had been partially mended in the next generation.

Later, I believe, Grandma and Grandpa met this young family at Walton, but I very much doubt if Tom and Ted ever met again.

THE LAST YEARS

IN THE early thirties, Grandma Shafe, who was then just in her seventies, fell ill and went to be nursed by her only daughter, Eva, who lived at Palmers Green.

Eva had one child, a schoolboy called Reg, to whom Grandma was devoted, and it was a very happy household.

Grandpa Shafe stayed on at Walton. No doubt it seemed prudent to keep the house going in the hope that Grandma's health would improve and that she would be able to return. Unfortunately, it was not to be. She died in 1933 at the age of seventy-three.

Grandpa lived for another two years, tended to the last by Eva, the only child of his four whom he truly loved.

I look back upon my two grandmothers with deep affection and admiration.

Neither had enjoyed an easy life, and when I first became conscious of them, they had just survived one of the most appalling wars known to mankind.

Nevertheless, they were always patient, kindly and laughter-loving, and it is perhaps this last quality of facing life with humour and zest which gave both my grandmothers that aura of warm happiness which they shared so bountifully with their grandchildren.

TIME
REMEMBERED

To
My Schoolfellows
of 1921–1924

CONTENTS

Foreword   105

Brave New World   107

The Village School   116

Facing the Unknown   122

Settling Down   131

Exploring   140

A Reluctant Musician   146

Beginning to Question   154

Perils and Pastimes   161

Work and Play   169

Pageants and People   180

Epilogue   191

And time remembered is grief forgotten,
And frosts are slain and flowers begotten.
From *Atalanta in Calydon*
A. C. SWINBURNE 1837–1909

Foreword

Tʜɪꜱ ɪꜱ ᴀɴ unashamedly nostalgic account of one of the happiest periods of my life. It dwells on that happiness, which is why Swinburne's quotation is used here.

It was a time which shaped the pattern of my future. It brought home to me the need to live in the country, to relish the changing seasons, village diversities, and to revere those writers whose particular genius was their interpretation of English country things – Thomas Hardy, W. H. Hudson, Flora Thompson, Edward Thomas, John Betjeman, and a score more.

The impact which those three years at a Kentish village school made upon me was unusually strong – one might almost say violent – for two reasons.

First, I was at that stage of life, not quite eight years old, when one is sharply aware of one's surroundings. It is at this stage in a child's development that imagination is at its most intense, and when witches, ghosts and giants take the place of Peter Rabbit in one's reading, and when woods and secret places take on a new and thrilling intimacy. I was more than ready.

The second reason was that I had suddenly exchanged the pressure of London life for the slower ways of the country, and it suited me. I had always loathed crowds, to the point of panic, and to go shopping with my mother, pressed against counters by towering adults, was sheer misery.

Knowing only one school, from the age of four, I assumed that all schools were large, noisy and regimented, with classes of fifty or more to a room. Moreover, I imagined that pressure to strive, to push on to even more arduous efforts, was common to all schools.

As an unambitious child, I disliked this wearisome régime. I had no desire to do better than my neighbours, and lacked any envy of their abilities, looks or possessions. I soon realized that what I really wanted was time to ruminate, time to observe, and often time to be alone.

At Chelsfield I came into my own, and have never ceased to be thankful.

BRAVE NEW WORLD

ON THE second day of March 1921 I went with my mother to Hither Green station in South London to go to our new home.

We were bound for Chelsfield, only a few stations down the line, and I looked forward eagerly to the journey. It was a weekday, and I really should have been in school, which made the whole adventure more exciting.

I was seven years old.

In those days of the London South-Eastern and Chatham Railway the trains were steam ones, and there was something awe-inspiring about the snorting throbbing engines which made the whole station shudder when they drew in to the platform.

Smoke puffed from the chimney, and steam gushed from various points along the side of the monster. Doors clanged, porters yelled, whistles blew, flags waved – the din was tremendous. The greasy step up into the third-class carriage was almost too high for a child to mount, but we were soon ensconced on the mottled red and black seats, and able to lean back and admire the photographs of distant resorts arranged just under the luggage rack.

Should I ever see the Leys at Folkestone, and those svelte ladies walking there, with their long skirts sweeping the grass and their elaborate hats needing a gloved hand clamped on them to withstand the sea breeze? Would I ever be lucky enough to see the Toad Stone at Tunbridge Wells, or the Esplanade at Margate?

As we chuffed slowly out of the station, I could see my old school, a three-storey building of brick with stone ornamentation, identical to many others put up by the London County Council.

I had started on the ground floor there, one of many 'Mixed Infants', but fortunate in that my Aunt Rose was one of the teachers, and had taken me to school in the early days. Later, I was elevated to the second floor 'Girls' where I shared a classroom with about fifty other six- and seven-year-olds and had 'real work' to do.

The boxes of beads, the wet clay balls, the sand trays and singing games were left behind. Now the day began in the classroom, after morning assembly in the hall, with ferocious attacks on multiplication tables.

Our teacher was called Miss Sanders, and that was how you addressed her. She seemed to me to be quite as old as my dear Grandma Read, but I doubt if she was more than thirty.

The blackboard was covered in columns of multiplication tables, and we began by chanting in unison.

> Four ones are four
> Four twos are eight
> Four threes are twelve
> Four fours are sixteen

and so on, until we reached the crescendo of

> Four tens are FORTY

Then the diminuendo:

> Four elevens are forty-four
> Four twelves are forty-eight.

Then we sank back. But not for long. Within seconds, Miss Sanders' red-tipped pointer would be scampering about the column while we blundered after it, faint but pursuing.

'Four sevens, four sevens, four sevens!' our teacher would yell.

'Twenty-eight!' we shouted back.

'Seven fours!' would continue our mentor fortissimo. The response would be less robust. Could seven fours be the same as four sevens? It seemed that it could.

We laboured on. Later generations would work it all out with milk bottles or Cuisenaire rods, but I doubt if any of them could match us for a completely instantaneous reaction to such challenges as 'Nine eights' in years to come.

We did an awful lot of chanting in those days, and rather liked it. Spellings, days of the week, months of the year, counting to a hundred in ones and then in twos, and sometimes in tens. We chanted a money table which began:

> Four farthings one penny

and ended with the triumphant shout:

> Twenty-one shillings one guinea.

And we learnt a new poem every week. (Although why seven-year-olds should be given that heart-breaking poem of Keats' beginning: 'I had a dove and the sweet dove died', I now wonder. It haunts me still.)

At playtime, in the bare asphalt wastes, there were literally hundreds of us milling about. We 'Mixed Infants' shared the space with the big girls, and watched in admiration as they skipped together chanting:

> R. White's Ginger Beer
> Goes off POP!

or 'Salt, Mustard, Vinegar, Pepper' followed by counting,

sometimes up to the forties or fifties, unless some duffer tripped up, amidst the groans of her fellows, and stopped the twirling rope.

There were tops, too, chalked with patterns, and whipped energetically along the asphalt with a string or leather thong on the end of a stick. Top-spinners were always in a frenzy and could be quite ferocious if one tripped over their treasure and wrecked its progress.

The noise naturally was horrendous, and it was almost a relief to hear the whistle blow and scurry into lines ready for marching indoors again.

'You will be going to Chelsfield School,' I had been told by my parents. I assumed that it would be much the same – large, noisy, busy with children, and ruled by some dozen or so teachers exhorting one to sit up, to stand straight, to stop sucking one's pencil, to work harder, to be neat, to be polite, and to be obedient. That, I took it, was what all schools were like. I felt I could face it after three years of the experience.

We chugged along steadily through Grove Park, leafy Chislehurst and Orpington. Here a vociferous porter just outside our window yelled: 'Orpington! Orping-ton! This train for Chelsfield! Knockholt, Dunton Green and Sevenoaks! Change at Dunton Green for Chevening 'Alt, Brasted and Westerrum!'

'Chelsfield next stop,' said my mother.

I was glad to hear it. It had been a long haul, I thought, between Chislehurst and Orpington through flat fields and with not much to see. It was years later that Petts Wood came to be built on that marshy ground, and then houses covered the fields I saw on my first journey, not only there but further down the line as well.

So far, all the stations had been fairly busy, despite the fact that it was late morning and the heaviest traffic had gone. I expected stations to be busy. Until then, my railway trips had been largely up the line from Hither Green to Charing Cross, usually in the company of my maiden Aunts Rose and Jess en route to the theatre or to do some shopping.

They, with my bachelor Uncle Harry, lived at 267 Hither Green Lane with my much-loved Grandma Read. I was going to miss them all.

Even more, I was already missing the companionship of my sister Lil, then aged ten, and staying for the rest of that spring term at Hither Green Lane in order to sit a scholarship examination which would determine her future. I should see her at the weekends and when she broke up. In the summer term, no doubt, she would accompany me to the village school before moving to higher things in September.

My father had stayed behind to supervise the packing, but was to catch a later train, which accounted for this rare experience of having my mother to myself.

The high embankment changed to a lower level, until we began to run between chalk cuttings. We were nearly there now and my mother prepared to descend from the train.

It drew up with a squealing of brakes, and a hissing of steam. We climbed down, carrying our one piece of luggage, a basket with a picnic lunch in it, and I stood dumbfounded.

There was no one on the platform except for the guard of the train. I had never seen a station like this. There were no posters, no trolleys, no litter bins, no milk churns! Furthermore, once the train had pulled away, everything was still and quiet.

Before me, on a green bank, sheltered from the wind, primroses were growing, and somewhere, high above, birds were singing, which I learnt soon after were skylarks, indigenous to this chalky North Downs country.

We crossed by a footbridge, our footsteps echoing hollowly, to the up platform. Here things were much more station-like to my eyes. There was a shirt-sleeved porter,

metal posters advertising Waverley pens and Nestlé's milk. There was even a chocolate machine where a penny would buy a bar of the delicious stuff.

The porter took our tickets and pointed out the way to our destination. It led across the station yard, through a gate, and on to a footpath beside a wood.

The train by now was well inside the tunnel beneath the North Downs on its way to Knockholt station. The peace of a spring morning enveloped us as we climbed the gentle slope, the wood on our right, and the deep railway cutting on our left.

We were both glad to stop now and again to have a rest. My mother had been ill, which was the main reason for our move, and I too had not long recovered from a bout of the Spanish influenza which had plagued Europe at the end of the First World War.

The wood gave way to fields of springy turf which made a pleasant resting place. There was a sturdy black metal sign set just inside the wires separating the railway property from our path. It said:

Trespassers will be fined £2.

It seemed a pity, as already a few early blue violets could be seen there. However, there was enough to enchant us on this side of the fence.

Tiny plants, which I should recognize later as sheep's-bit scabious and thyme, were being pressed under my legs. The larks were in joyous frenzy above. The sky was blue, the now distant wood misty with early buds, and the air was heady to a London child.

A great surge of happiness engulfed me. This is where I was going to live. I should learn all about birds and trees and flowers. This is where I belonged. Any qualms about a new school vanished in these surroundings.

This was the country, and I was at home there.

It was a knowledge that was to stay throughout my life.

THE VILLAGE SCHOOL

Two days later, my mother took me to the village school to be admitted as a pupil.

It was a rainy morning and I wore my new mackintosh. In those days, little girls had a garment, rather like Red Riding Hood's in shape, consisting of a rubber cape with a hood. The latter could be drawn up round the head and had a minuscule frill all round one's face. Those mackintoshes certainly kept out the rain, which is more than you can say for some of our present-day raincoats, but they were airless and hot.

It was almost a mile and a quarter to the school, along a lane already showing few yellow coltsfoot and celandine flowers on the banks, and a thickening of buds on some large and ancient trees which I soon discovered were elm and walnut.

We passed an ivy-covered farmhouse called Julian Brimstone Farm. There was a large yard beside it, and a wall of flint and brick separated it from the road. We paused for a minute to admire the rain-pocked pond where ducks and geese were busy about their affairs.

The stables were being cleaned out, steam rising from the dung. The few cart horses were out at work in the fields.

We passed the church on our left, standing well back from the road. A row of lime trees led to it. Then the lane passed under a splendid row of ancient elm trees, sloped gently downhill, and we were in the village street.

The first building on the right was a cream-painted shed. This was the Fire Station and housed, I learnt later, a small machine which could be pushed along by hand and trundled to any local outbreak of fire. Rumour had it that, on one of the rare occasions when it was used, the hose was found to be perished and spouted water freely all along its length, and not from the nozzle.

The small building was well embedded in a hawthorn hedge, which no doubt offered sanctuary to many a nesting bird.

Almost opposite stood a flint cottage where there lived a German couple called Ulrich. He was something of an artist and designed the black and white drawing on the parish magazine showing St Martin's church.

There were three shops on the right-hand side, and a public house called 'The Five Bells' where our lane met another. And here I had my first view of my new school.

I could not believe my eyes. Where was the great three-storey building of red brick? Where was the vast expanse of playground?

Here before me was a one-storey building with a slate roof. Steps led up to the small playground, and a row of pollarded lime trees towered above the railings. On climbing the steps we could then see some sturdy wooden benches set under the trees.

The first door had BOYS written above it, so we went round the building to the back, and entered by a door

marked GIRLS. Presumably 'Mixed Infants' used this door too.

It was very quiet in the lobby, and there was no one to be seen. My mother knocked on the glass of a nearby door, and a pleasant young woman came out and said that if we would wait a moment she would tell the headmaster that we were there.

A *headmaster*? I was appalled. At my old school, we saw no male teachers, and the ruler of that distant world had been Miss Pope, a headmistress of great dignity. I had heard my Aunt Rose speak of her with due deference, and now and again she entered our classrooms and we all stood up respect-fully. It was she who took assembly in the morning, and gave us important pieces of instruction such as urging us each to bring a handkerchief, or telling us that the Great War had ended which was why the Union Jack was flying from the flag-pole.

But a *headmaster*! Did this mean that boys and girls would all be mixed together, as in my Infants' days? I peered through the glass of the classroom door, and there indeed were boys and girls, much about my age, sitting in desks, although it seemed that two boys appeared to share a desk, and two girls another, so that at least one would have the comfort of sitting beside a *girl* evidently, and not a *boy*.

While we waited in the lobby among the damp coats and hats, a little girl emerged from another door and skipped up to the wash basin. There were two basins, but one was broken, and remained so, I remember, for months. There was a brass tap which gave only cold water, and this little imp set about washing her hands with a piece of yellow Sunlight soap, grey and grainy with age.

We smiled at each other. My first encounter with one of my schoolfellows cheered me.

'Hullo,' she said. 'Miss Smiff sent me out.' It sounded as though she might be in disgrace, but she showed no sign of distress. In fact, she hummed cheerfully as she endeavoured to create a lather, and then wiped her hands on a damp towel hanging nearby.

She beamed again. 'Goodbye! Got to get back,' she volunteered, and skipped back to her classroom, as Mr Clarke the headmaster appeared and beckoned us in. He was a squarely-built man of medium height, with dark eyes and black hair. His voice was pleasant, his expression kind. I liked him at once.

We went through the classroom of the first

teacher we had met, and were introduced to her. She was Miss Ellis, and smiled nicely. I was very conscious of many eyes behind me, no doubt examining me from hair to toes.

In the headmaster's room, beyond the glass and pine partition, more eyes watched us. Here the boys and girls were older, some almost grown up, it seemed to me. The oldest must have been a venerable fourteen.

Mr Clarke began to write down the particulars of my age, past schooling and so on, and my mother went through the usual ritual of spelling our surname S-H-A-F-E, which always flummoxed new acquaintances.

Meanwhile, I gazed about the room, noting a fine open fire protected by a cage-like fireguard. Along its brass top, a row of knitted gloves steamed gently.

 There were some large wooden cupboards, and one glass-fronted one with an interesting-looking collection of books. (They turned out to be remarkably dreary, as it happened.) The windows were high, but a few fish-paste jars stood on the windowsills, holding early primroses and violets.

In this room, too, each desk held two children of the same sex. Exercise books were open before them, and pens were in hand, but naturally work was suspended while my mother and I were there to be scrutinised.

At length, the headmaster took us to the door, telling Miss Ellis, in passing, that I should be in her class.

This time, we went through the boys' lobby, said our farewells to Mr Clarke, descended the steps to the village street, and began the long walk home.

I wonder now why I was not left there that day, but there must have been some good reason. In any case, it was very pleasant to have a few hours' breathing space, and to mull over in my mind the first impressions of this extraordinary place which bore no resemblance to my idea of a school.

'Do you think you will like it?' my mother asked when we were halfway home.

'Yes,' I said with conviction.

I suspect, on looking back, that she had some doubts about the type of education I should receive there. She too was accustomed to the ways of large town schools, and knew from her teacher sister Rose the high standards of attainment expected from the pupils, and the relentless pressure kept up to ensure scholastic success. Payment-by-results was not all that far behind in the teaching profession in those days, and class teachers were on their mettle to prove their worth.

I had plenty to think about. I remembered those watching eyes, boys' alarmingly strange, as well as girls'. There was not one person among them that I knew. No Aunt Rose would be with me as a protector, either on the long journey to school and back, or in that queer quiet little building I had just left. And my sister, too, was now far away.

I should be alone, and a stranger, in a completely different world.

Facing The Unknown

Opposite Julian Brimstone Farm stood a pair of farm cottages, and in one of them lived a young family called Whitehead. The father worked for the local farmer, not the one who lived at Julian Brimstone Farm, but a much larger landowner whose acres lay on the other side of the road. One of his fields was opposite our own house.

Incidentally, it was in this field one day in the late twenties that I heard a little boy walking round the edge, rattling a tin with stones in it and singing hoarsely:

> O all you blackytops
> Keep off my master's crops
> Here I come
> With my big gun
> La-la-la-la-la-la.

He could not have been more than nine years of age.

Dan Whitehead was fair, of ruddy complexion and cheerful. His wife was tall with very dark eyes and black hair, a handsome woman.

She agreed very kindly to my mother's request that her daughter Hilda might 'look after me' on the journey to and from school, at least for the first few days. We became firm friends.

Her little brother Billy was too young then to come to school, but Hilda had had her share of minding children and was conscientious in looking after me. I was exceedingly glad of her company.

I got to know that mile-and-a-quarter journey very well, for I made it four times a day. In that first spring it was Hilda who showed me where the beds of violets grew, some white and sweet-smelling, some dog violets of blue, and one rare bed of pink ones whose whereabouts we kept secret.

She also showed me a blackbird's nest near her gate not far from a patch of snowberries whose white globes enchanted us later in the year.

Every morning we called at Hilda's grandmother's house, one of a pair of clapboarded cottages a little further along the lane. I was rather afraid of the old lady, for although she was kind, and later invited us to pick gooseberries in an old overgrown orchard at the end of her garden, she had an appalling cough, and looked so ill when caught in one of its paroxysms that I feared she would die in front of me.

Hilda took all this in her stride, and we collected there a small boy called Kenneth who was being fostered in the house.

In her grandmother's scullery was a fascinating green globe which stood in a jar of water. According to the old lady, it was a weather gauge, but I never understood how it worked.

Kenneth, like Shakespeare's schoolboy, 'crept unwillingly to school', and Hilda had to use all her wiles to get him there. We also collected a younger cousin of Hilda's on the way, so that we were quite a little band as we approached the village.

Between us, on our journey, we made wonderful discoveries. A robin had built a nest on a ledge inside a hollow damson tree, near the young cousin's house. A blackbird had another tucked among a tangle of honeysuckle, at the top of a steep bank. Luckily, it was close to a telegraph pole, which helped our climbing efforts on the way to inspect the nest. Good children that we were, we did not touch the eggs, but Hilda, experienced and wise, warned us not to tell any of 'the big boys'.

'They are *cruel*!' she assured us. 'I've seen some of them throw the little birds on the road and *stamp* on them!'

We were suitably horrified, and swore never to tell of our discoveries.

About halfway to school stood a great pile of grey flints ready for road mending. This, of course, we climbed and ran along, enjoying a heady glimpse of the fields beyond the top of the hedge.

Opposite, in that first year, there was a field of sage. I had never seen more than a wispy sprig or two in London gardens, and to see and smell a whole fieldful was an amazing experience.

Between the sage field and the church stood a splendid Georgian house called Court Lodge, but even more intriguing to us children was the lodge at its gates, for in the garden of this house stood a high pole to which was fixed a length of wire which ran to the roof of the house. It was my first introduction to a wireless aerial.

Later, we had one in our own garden, and a crystal set in the sitting-room, with headphones to listen to the crack- 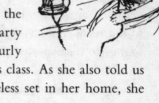 ling, and occasional voice, which emerged miraculously from all the paraphernalia.

A pretty girl, called Elsie, lived at the lodge and frequently joined our party on the way to school. She had curly auburn hair, and was in Mr Clarke's class. As she also told us something about the hallowed wireless set in her home, she was obviously treated with respect.

By this time, we were almost in the village and as we entered 'The Street', as the local people called it, we could see knots of children approaching from other directions. All were on foot. I don't remember even a bicycle being ridden by a child to school, and school buses, of course, were far in the future.

Some walked from Well Hill, a mile or so north of the village, some from an outpost to the west. A few came from scattered cottages on the road from the station. Miss Smith herself, the kindly ruler of the Infants' class for many years, came by train, and walked the lonely mile from there every school morning and back in the afternoon, in rain or shine.

Most of the houses in the village itself had children living in them. Some of the families were large. There were eight or nine offspring in one cottage close to the school, and a good many parents had four or five children.

As the school bell began to ring, the Divalls and Martins

emerged from their houses near Groom's, the baker; the Sparrowhawks from theirs near Neal's, the grocers; Margaret Smith from the Post Office; Harold and Violet Smith (no relation, incidentally) from a handsome clapboard house, and the Wickendens from another near by.

By the time the bell stopped, almost a hundred children had assembled. Mr Clarke appeared in the playground, lines were formed, and boys and girls, aged from five to fourteen, entered the lobbies to start another day.

On my first morning, it was soon apparent that this school bore no resemblance to my old one.

There, we had assembled for morning prayers in an enormous hall. Miss Pope had stood on a dias, resplendent in an ankle-length dove-grey frock, with a watch pinned over her heart, and a Bible on the table before her.

After singing the hymn and saying prayers, we all sat cross-legged on the floor to listen to a story from the Bible, and to take heed of any notices given out before returning to our classrooms. One of the staff played a march on the piano and we did our best to keep in time as we stomped away. Here, Mr Clarke stood in the doorway of the partition which divided standards one, two, three and four, from standards, five, six and seven, his own class. Miss Ellis sat at the piano hard by, and we sang a hymn, following the words from some rather scruffy hymn books which we had to share. The Infants, it seemed, attended to their devotions in their own classroom.

Prayers were said with bowed heads, Mr Clarke told us that he expected less noise in the playground than he had heard yesterday, the door was closed, and we sat down in our desks, ready for a Scripture lesson. Now I had time to look about me, as Miss Ellis began the story of Joseph and his brothers.

There was a large photograph of Queen Mary and King George V behind Miss Ellis's desk. He was ablaze with medals and decorations, a fine upstanding figure with a neat beard. His Queen was wasp-waisted in white lace, a star on her breast, her hair crisply waved. They were a handsome pair, I thought, and I was proud that my father had fought for them in France in the Royal Horse Artillery.

A large marmalade-coloured cupboard stood beside the photograph, and on its side hung a little board headed 'Attendance'. This was divided into five, one section for each school day of the week. One of the big boys from standard seven, I was to discover, came round in the morning and afternoon to count heads and to put the total on this little board.

There was a large open fire surrounded by a sturdy fireguard. I could feel its warmth from my seat in a front desk, shared with a little girl introduced to me as Rose.

Our desk was old and heavily scarred. It had two inkwells, one let into the middle and the other at the end. A groove ran from one to the other, and in it rested our pens, with lovely orange wooden holders. Mine had a new nib. Rose's had seen some wear.

There was a large blackboard propped on an easel, and Miss Ellis's chalk rested in a groove on the crossbar of this. When the Scripture lesson was over, she began to put up some addition and subtraction sums in hundreds, tens and units, and these I found I could do, although with some difficulty. Arithmetic was not my strong point, but my early schooling carried me through, and the fact that I knew my tables inside out concealed the knowledge that this was about all I did know of the subject.

At playtime I rushed to find Hilda. Rose accompanied us, and Margaret from the Post Office was friendly, and showed me the gap where her tooth had just come out. I much appreciated the honour, and tried to hide my horror at the sight.

It was after play that my first problem arrived.

'Take out your writing books,' said Miss Ellis. She handed me a brand new one, and then turned to the blackboard.

I forget what she wrote but whatever it was, it was inscribed in copperplate. I could not read it, let alone copy it. At my old school, we had been taught to print – 'to do script', as it was called – with each letter separate from the next.

I watched Rose dip in her pen and start to copy the elaborate rigmarole. Despair engulfed me.

'Get on, dear,' said Miss Ellis. 'I can't,' I faltered. 'I've only done script!'

'We done that in the Infants,' said an insufferable boy in the next row.

'When we had pencils,' contributed another smug child.

Miss Ellis took charge, and ushered me to her desk with my pristine writing book. Every eye was upon us.

'Just show me how you write,' she said encouragingly, and waved towards the incomprehensible scribble on the board.

'I can't read it,' I confessed, now near to tears.

'It says: "March comes in like a lion and goes out like a lamb." You can use my inkwell.'

I did so, and standing at her desk printed the sentence in my best script.

As I finished, the door opened and in came Mr Clarke. Miss Ellis rose and the two had a whispered conversation above my head.

Mr Clarke took up my book.

'She can't do real writing,' said the
insufferable boy smugly.
'But you can read every word,'
retorted Mr Clarke, 'which is more
than I can say about your scrawl!'
I loved him from that moment.

SETTLING DOWN

Looking back, I now realize how lucky I was to arrive in Chelsfield at just that time.

Although the village was only seventeen miles from Charing Cross, and a mere two miles from the main London to Hastings road, it remained a close-knit rural community.

Most of the wage-earners worked on the farms, although two or three fine houses, such as Court Lodge, provided domestic employment for several more. There were two bakeries in the village and a grocer's shop, and those two had one or two local men acting as indoor helpers or drivers of the delivery vans. One baker still delivered his bread in a high gig, with a spanking bay horse to draw it.

It was a fruit-growing area, strawberries being one of the main crops. Gooseberries and raspberries also did well, and later in the year the orchards produced excellent apples, pears and plums. There were no hops grown in our village, but extensive hop fields were cultivated some miles south towards the Weald of Kent.

Our school holidays were sensibly adapted to the seasons, for as well as short holidays at Christmas and Easter, we had a three-week fruit-picking holiday in early July, and a three-week hop-picking holiday in September. It was this acknowledgement of Nature's importance and its direct influence on rural economy which gave me such delight.

The seasons, when I lived in London, had small effect on one's life. Certainly, clothes had to be warmer in winter, the muffin man rang his bell, and the coal cart was a regular feature of the winter scene, just as the water cart, with its sprinkler, was a sign of summer. But in a town school, one was hardly aware of the change of the seasons. Holidays came at Christmas and Easter, and the main one in August when our family went to Walton-on-the-Naze to stay with my grandparents, and to share the windswept beach with other children also on holiday.

I relished the change to breaks in July and September when the country was full of interest. Shabby August, with its drying grass and end-of-summer feeling, might just as well be spent in school where I grew increasingly happy.

My early fears, particularly of the boys, whose company had virtually vanished when I became a Big Girl at the age of six in my old school, now disappeared. It was true that they teased me, but I could take that cheerfully, used as I was to my father's bantering ways. In any case, I soon found that the girls were very motherly, and would rush to the assistance of any young thing being persecuted.

On the whole, they were a well-mannered pleasant set of children whose parents would not brook disrespect, disobedience or bad language. Most of us went either to the parish church of St Martin's or to the Wesleyan chapel which stood opposite the school. Mr Clarke, the kindest of men, nevertheless stood no nonsense from his pupils, and the cane stood in readiness for those whose behaviour merited its attention. All of us knew our limits, and if we were foolish or bold enough to kick over the traces, we knew what was in store. It all contributed to a peaceful and well-ordered society.

I might well have been bullied for I was definitely the odd one, a lone stranger amidst these closely-knit children, many of whom had known each other from birth. Apart from their general good nature and my own resilience, I unwittingly found another way to make friends.

On my previous birthday, I had been given a scooter which I loved dearly. It was a simple affair of a wooden platform and an upright wooden column which sprouted two handles. With one's left foot on the platform and one's right foot pushing energetically at the ground, a fair turn of speed could be enjoyed. Downhill, of course, it was utter bliss, and my sister, who also had one, demonstrated this by standing on her scooter at the top of the hill outside our house, and rushing down the steep quarter of a mile to the main London road, without needing to put a foot to the ground. We played this game down the steep slope of the North Downs until our parents discovered it and forbade us to go right to the traffic at the bottom so that, much to our chagrin, we were obliged to put our feet down some fifty yards short of our target.

At the head of the hill, opposite our house, was a notice board which warned carters about the steepness of the hill before them, and exhorting them not to attempt it unless 'with a properly adjusted skidpan'.

I think our right shoes acted as our skidpans for they were always worn through well before the left ones.

Miss Ellis gave me permission to bring my scooter to school, and I pounded along in fine style, little thinking of the effect it would have on my schoolfellows.

I had made the journey alone that morning, and as soon as I rattled into the village I was surrounded by admiring children. The boys were particularly interested and asked deferentially if they could 'have a go'. They took turns in scooting up and down the pavement below the school wall, while I sat on the steps and watched.

The school bell rang whilst the fun continued. When it stopped, the boys lugged it up the steps for me, begging me to let them have turns again at playtime. My star was certainly in the ascendant, and I was in the rare position of being able to state my terms.

As is happened, my scooter was banned from the playground, although I was allowed to keep it in an obscure corner of the lobby, and ride it to and from school. Needless to say, I had an accompaniment of entreating schoolfellows whenever I had my scooter with me.

In my early days at Chelsfield School, my scooter was hard-worked, partly, I suspect, because of the influence it gave me over my schoolfellows, but also because that summer in 1921 was one of endless sunshine and, consequently, quite severe drought.

I remember a straw hat which my mother made me wear. It was a boater shape, with a ribbon band of pale pink with pale blue spots. The ends hung down behind, a little longer than my hair (with fringe), and streamed behind as I scorched along on my trusty scooter. The hat was anchored by elastic under the chin.

My cotton frocks were cut in Magyar style, the short sleeves cut in one with the straight front and back, and a scooped or squared neckline. These, no doubt, were run up by my dressmaker, dear Aunt Jess, whom I had left behind at 267 Hither Green Lane with Grandma Read.

These cotton frocks had knickers to match which was considered very avant-garde by my contemporaries. That summer I wore no socks, just leather sandals, the right one soon becoming dilapidated by friction with the gritty road. I don't think I ever realized the freedom of loose, light clothing so much as I did in that scorching summer. As a small child, I had worn a vest, chemise, petticoat, knickers, frock and pinafore. It was wonderful to have shed so many superfluous layers.

One would have thought that with so much clothing discarded by my mother, that over-powering hat would have gone the same way. But, in those days, heads seemed to have been considered particularly vulnerable to weather in all its variety, so hats were deemed absolutely essential. Most of my schoolfriends sported plain linen affairs, which I thought very smart and practical. But as my own large straw was much admired by quite big girls of ten or more, I grew fonder of it in time.

Most of the girls in that hot summer wore frocks made of cotton check gingham or flowered print, but knickers were mostly white with elastic at waist and leg, although a few children still wore white cotton drawers buttoned on to a Liberty bodice. Pinafores too were still worn by one or two girls, and in the March of my arrival when winter clothes were the rule, white pinafores, black stockings and laced-up black boots were the accepted wear by some of the girls.

Hair was worn long, either in plaits or drawn back and tied up in a bow on the crown of the head. A little later, the 'American Bob' hairstyle became the thing, a great saving in hair ribbons and celluloid hair-slides which were always getting lost or broken.

The boys of my age were in shorts, usually of grey flannel, and jerseys with collars, shirt-style. In the hot weather, they wore short-sleeved cotton shirts. I much admired their striped belts which fastened with a snake's-head buckle.

Those elderly gentlemen of thirteen and fourteen in Mr Clarke's class were clad in long trousers, some I suspect, adapted from their father's cast-offs. What with long trousers, breaking voices, and such important duties as counting heads morning and afternoon, not to mention collecting traysful of inkwells, it is no wonder that we small fry beyond the partition looked upon them as practically Mr Clarke's contemporaries.

They were held in some respect, and on the whole were a good influence on us younger ones. Within a year or so, they would be out in the world, the majority following their fathers into agricultural work, but some to take up work in carpenters' shops or garages. One or two would go into the Army, but very few would go on to higher education.

I cannot recall any boy winning a scholarship to the local grammar school. Times were still hard after the 1914–18 war, and were to become harder still as the Depression approached. Agriculture was in a sad way, and most country families needed every penny that could be brought in by their wage-earners. The boys themselves seemed ready and eager at fourteen to get out into the world, and as far as one could see, had no regrets about abandoning 'school-learning'.

They were not great readers although the girls seemed to be. When they left school, the latter would probably find their chief relaxation in books borrowed, as likely as not, from the splendid libraries which Kent County Council provided very early. Our family had particular cause to be grateful for this excellent service for we were all avid readers, and paid a weekly visit to the Reading Room to rummage through the library box for new treasures.

One of my library books, *Twelve Stories and a Dream* by H. G. Wells, I remember particularly vividly as Tony, our adored mongrel dog, chewed it up and we were obliged to pay some horrific sum – I think it was four shillings – for its replacement.

Our school library was poor. One or two adventure stories by Henty and R. L. Stevenson seemed to be the boys' sustenance, and I believe Louisa M. Alcott was provided for us girls. But almost all of one of the three shelves was taken up by a row of identical grey-covered books with the title *Thrift*. They must have been presented to the school by some earnest society intent on educating the poor, but in fact they were as grey inside as out, completely unreadable, and fit only for the pulping machine.

Mr Clarke was generous in lending books from his own shelves, and I recall ploughing through his copy of *David Copperfield* which my mother insisted must be shrouded in brown paper, whilst in my care, to protect it.

We had one or two readers in our desks, mostly composed of extracts from Goldsmith, Shakespeare, Scott and the like. There was a dearth of humorous writing, and very little poetry. Most of the latter was learnt by rote in the lower junior classes under Miss Ellis's supervision, and I suspect that the school leavers, as a whole, had only these remnants to cheer them through life.

In Mr Clarke's class, we were given a poetry book occasionally, and told to learn a poem. Some of the girls did this conscientiously, and I know that I learnt Walter de la Mare's enchanting poem 'Nod' at that time. It is with me still.

To test our poetical knowledge, Mr Clarke sometimes called out a child at random to recite. The boys, to a man, reeled off that rather dreadful poem of Wordworth's:

> The cock is crowing
> The stream is flowing
> The small birds twitter
> The lake doth glitter (etc.)

which they had been compelled to learn years earlier. Somehow, they always got away with it, and we girls, who had been industrious, were rightly incensed.

But when it came to singing, the school came into its own. We were well drilled in Tonic Solfa, the narrow strip of shiny material draped over the blackboard and our teacher's red-tipped pointer bounding up and down from Doh-to-Soh-to-Doh while we sang to its demands.

Mr Clarke had a superb bass voice, almost as velvety dark as Paul Robeson's, and led us surely through the intricacies of *The National Song Book*, with Miss Ellis accompanying on the piano.

We really enjoyed singing lessons, and probably our favourite was 'Charlie Is My Darling', for we were all impressed by one of the big boys who was kind, good-looking and already a charmer, and whose name was Charlie.

We sang it with all the fervour of youthful admiration rather than ardour for the Jacobite cause. And if Mr Clarke knew what lay behind our fortissimo rendering, as surely he did, he gave no sign.

Exploring

THE EASTER holiday brought my sister Lil home for good, much to our mutual pleasure.

Unlike some sisters separated by three years in age, we always got on well together. Naturally, we had our fights too. Lil was much cleverer than I was in these encounters, and one of her subtlest moves, when I was about five and had just mastered garter stitch, was to do a row of purl knitting on my plain-knitted doll's scarf. Powerless to unravel it, and yet loathing this wrong line in my painfully-acquired inch of work, I could only yell with rage – or I may have bitten her. I was rather good at biting when young.

Occasionally we had fights over our dolls, usually if we were playing schools with them. They sat in a row, usually propped against the fender, and were given arithmetic tests

set, I need hardly say, by Lil. We were supposed to 'do' our own dolls' papers, and as Lil's mathematical ability was always outstanding, and mine just the opposite, my poor charges invariably failed, and Lil's succeeded brilliantly.

However, I retaliated later by jumping out unexpectedly, preferably in darkness from handy cupboards or corners, and frightening my sister into quaking terror. I found this ruse very satisfactory.

During those first summer months, we explored our new surroundings, enjoying each other's company after our brief separation.

The garden was still in the making. Flower beds were being dug by my father, and a vegetable patch. A tennis court was also laid out, and one or two chicken houses complete with runs were set up.

My father, in common with a lot of men after the war, was deluded enough to imagine that a small fortune could be made from chicken-farming. He soon found that it was one of the quickest roads to penury, but at least we always had plenty of eggs to eat.

But it was outside our garden gate that we found most of our excitement.

There was a roadside pond almost opposite our house. In the early spring it was awash with frogs' spawn, I was to discover, but even now, in April, it had its charms. Trees grew around three sides, mostly scrubby hawthorns, but there was one large tree, probably a crab apple or wild cherry, which we could climb. Here we found a perch, and watched the occasional passer-by who had no knowledge of his hidden and delighted watchers.

The pond was not large enough to harbour moorhens or mallard, but homely birds like blackbirds and starlings, or a flutter of squabbling little tabby sparrows, came to drink and splash in the shallows, and we were entranced.

Halfway down the steep hill, a cart track led off which ended in a south-facing field heavily hedged. These hedges yielded more joy, for under them grew sheets of blue violets, many of them sweet-smelling, and a little later spangles of white stitchwort whose seedpods could be popped with great satisfaction.

One hedge was composed of bullace bushes, that round pale green wild fruit which is scarce these days. Later that year, we picked basketsful of these little plums, and made pounds of scarlet jelly, sharp to the taste, which made a welcome addition to the larder shelves.

During that summer we discovered wild strawberries, dog roses, honeysuckle, bryony, wild hops and scores of other delights in that field, some appealing to taste, or scent, or simply enchanting the eye with colour and form.

But even more exciting was the wood which lay beyond it. It was one of those pleasant and welcoming oak and hazel woods, now becoming rare, giving way as they have to the sinister conifer plantations to be seen dominating so much of our countryside.

Our wood was light. The sunshine shone through the

leaves upon clumps of primroses, and later the sea of bluebells whose scent was everywhere.

Underfoot, the ground was soft with the leaf mould of centuries. Plenty of rabbits burrowed here, or skittered away at our approach with a glimpse of white scuts. Now and again, a squirrel could be seen leaping airily, a puff of grey smoky fur, in the branches overhead. And always there were birds. Wood pigeons clattered from the oak trees, blackbirds fled squawking from the bramble bushes, tits collected the swinging caterpillars from their gossamer threads to carry to their young, and scores of birds unseen rustled among the dead leaves or stirred the young bracken.

Every visit to the wood brought fresh discoveries. In one clearing, a gigantic beech tree grew on a sandy slope. This provided massive low branches, grey and crinkled like elephant skin, upon which we sat, bouncing up and down with the wind in our hair.

We found a yew tree not far away which soon became our particular headquarters. It was easy to climb, and we would sit aloft in its aromatic fastness, picking at the trunk to uncover its pink fleshiness, and relishing the comfort of its rough support and the glossy beauty of its foliage.

Sometimes we brought our dolls to enjoy the pleasures of the wood. We would make diminutive jellies or tiny sandwiches for them, and give them a picnic in some particularly favoured glade. Tony, the dog, always accompanied us although he resented being left below the trees we climbed, and mooched about, whining pathetically at being deserted.

On one occasion, when my sister and I and another little friend called Peggy were taking our ease, high in the yew tree, there was the crack of an air gun, and Tony, far below, began yelping in terror.

As one man, yelping ourselves, we crashed down through the branches, knickers, Liberty bodices, skirts, hair, all drawn upwards, to confront a startled man with a light gun. He was looking white and shaken as well he might, at the sight of three such vociferous little girls.

'You ought to look at what you're shooting at!' screamed Peggy, scarlet-faced, and the superbly ungrammatical sentence, and its intonation, has stayed with me over the years.

Tony was engulfed in our loving embraces. There was a slight smear of blood on his chest where the pellet had grazed him, but this did not stop the dog from making the most of his troubles, and I remember we took turns in carrying him home, after berating the man soundly, threatening him with police, fathers, the RSPCA and any other relevant authority we could call to mind.

Tony lay on his back, his four legs stiffly in the air, as we bore him homeward. He weighed a ton, and after having disinfectant dabbed on his wound, recovered immediately at the sight of his dinner plate.

Looking back now, some sixty-odd years on, I suppose the man had been out to get a rabbit for the larder, saw a movement and took a pot shot. The sudden descent of three wrathful children, falling from the heavens, must have made him glad that he had not let fly at a pigeon, or any other animal near our lofty perch. He was certainly a very frightened man.

The pond, the hazel wood, the fields and hedgerows provided us with a thousand marvels. An old chalk-pit, across a nearby field, gave us endless pleasure as we slid down the slopes to the detriment of our clothes. Downland country is always at its best in summer, and that never-to-be-forgotten spell of brilliant sunshine, week after week, gilded the long outdoor days, burnished our town-bred limbs, bleached our hair, and illumined our memories for ever.

Only streams were lacking in that part of the North Downs, but later we found the thrill of running water when we walked to Shoreham in the Darent valley, some four miles away, the village immortalised by Samuel Palmer. Later still, as we grew older, bolder and stronger, we explored more of those lovely villages, Otford, Brasted and Chevening, carrying our picnic lunches, and bringing home the gold of kingcups, exotic trophies from a foreign land.

A RELUCTANT MUSICIAN

DURING that summer term, Lil and I went to school together. I don't think the impact made upon my sister was very great. For one thing, she only spent one term there, and I spent ten.

But there was another good reason. Her thoughts were of the school ahead, and the results of the examination which she had sat recently. These obligatory weeks at the village school were of a temporary nature, and although the respite from town pressures must have been welcome, the school and its children were not to affect her as keenly as they did me.

News came during that term that she had been given a place at Blackheath High School, and the family rejoiced. Naturally, there was a great deal of preparation to be done, and there was a flurry of shopping for school uniform, black stockings, name tapes, shoe bags, a satchel, and so on. Although I was proud of her achievement, I was secretly glad that I was spared all this bother.

The biggest worry of all was how Lil was to get to this new school from Chelsfield. At that time, there was no bus along the main Hastings road to London and trains did not fit in. It was necessary to get to Farnborough where a 47 bus could be caught.

This was a good three miles from home, and mostly uphill. She would have to make the journey twice daily by bicycle as well as the bus trip. It meant a very early start in the mornings, which was not too awful in the summer, but the winter trips were formidable.

The fear of traffic and the fear of child molesters were minimal in those happier days, but my parents soon realized that the journey was really too much for a young girl, particularly as homework increased. In the end, Lil was transferred to a school in Bromley, a much more accessible place which could be reached by train, and later by bus.

Meanwhile, I settled happily to my carefree life. By now I had made several good friends. Besides Hilda, I relished the company of Margaret from the Post Office and particularly that of Norah Foreman whose father was a fruit farmer at Well Hill.

These friends sometimes came to tea, or I went to their homes, where we inspected each other's toys, exchanged books, dressed each other's dolls, or simply enjoyed the strange pleasures of a different house and garden.

My parents too began to make friends as soon as the early settling-in process was over. They both joined the church choir and the local Glee Club. Both were musical, and sang well, and my father had played the organ at church from the age of about fourteen or so. It was no wonder that they had insisted on piano lessons for their daughters at an early age when we lived in London.

My sister must have been eight or nine when these began, and she took to it like a duck to water. I, three years younger, went along with her and had the basics taught me. I loathed it.

These lessons took place in a house quite near our own at Lewisham, and I only remember a rather stuffy room with a

circular sofa, covered in red plush, where I sat whilst Lil practised scales, arpeggios and the advanced end of Ezra Read's musical exercises. Needless to say, I hardly reached Page 3.

When we moved, I had hoped fondly that this torture would cease. Lil was to continue her musical studies at school, and it was my hope that any ambitions for me in that line would die a natural death.

However, a music teacher gave lessons in the village, and I was signed on. A more reluctant pupil poor Miss Hill never had.

She seemed to me a very old lady, small and afflicted with a spinal disability. She looked after her father, a handsome old gentleman who was probably then in his seventies, so that his daughter was probably then only in her forties.

She dressed in dark clothes and wore a gold chain and spectacles. She was exceedingly kind and patient, but kept a ruler at hand for tapping erring fingers. I knew that ruler well.

I progressed slowly and painfully through Ezra Read and can still play 'Sweet Memories' (to the mental accompaniment of Miss Hill's ruler). After that, new works were bought, one by one, and as they had to be sent for and despatched by post, I soon learnt a major delaying tactic.

There was something called Continental Fingering which showed the notes with 1, 2, 3, 4 or 5 above them. This, I professed, was impossible for me to follow, and I stuck out for English Fingering – always the patriot – which showed the thumb as a cross, and the fingers numbered 1 to 4. This, for some reason, always took longer to procure, so that I could rattle away for another week or two at Ezra Read or Reger, and save myself, and Miss Hill's ruler, a good deal of unnecessary activity.

After my half-hour's ordeal, Miss Hill gave me a cup of tea and a biscuit, and once, some Edinburgh rock, which was new to me and has remained a weakness of mine ever since. I was much intrigued by a paper cut-out ball, fixed to the ceiling, which she explained was 'the flies' playground' and which kept them away from the rest of the room in theory.

I grew very fond of Miss Hill as time passed. My lessons took place after school, and she would accompany me, after our tea party, along a grassy lane by the side of her house to a footpath across strawberry fields which gave me a quick way home.

The house was beautiful, built in Queen Anne's reign, and standing high above the road, as so many houses did in that village. The garden was composed of a number of flower beds surrounded by low box hedges, and here old Mr Hill would be strolling or sitting on a garden seat. He was always well wrapped up, a white silk muffler at his throat. I was particularly impressed with the way he took off his cap to me, displaying silvery hair, and gave me a courtly little bow. Not many people treated me so politely, and I much appreciated his courtesy.

One winter afternoon of bitter cold, it began to snow. Dusk was falling, and whirling snowflakes made it darker still. Miss Hill was much perturbed, and there was no way of getting in touch with my parents, for neither household had a telephone. I was quite game to strike out on my own, and rather looked forward to being part of the wild weather, but Miss Hill insisted on my sitting by the fire whilst she overcame the problem.

Luckily she remembered that Mr Stanley, the milkman, should be arriving, and as his farm was near my home, he would give me a lift.

I was wrapped up as carefully as a Christmas parcel, scarf arranged over my mouth and chin, and tied securely behind my back, whilst we awaited Mr Stanley.

When he came, the position was
explained to him and I was welcomed
on board his milk float. My music case
was stuffed under a shelf at the
front, Mr Stanley flicked his whip,
and Miss Hill waved from the
lighted doorway.

It was a blissful journey through
the flurry of snow. I stood up at the
front watching the flakes melt as they
landed on the pony's black back. We fairly
spanked along, the pony snorting and tossing
his head at this strange element and anxious
to get back to a warm stable.

It was the most exciting ride I had ever had. There was
nothing, I decided, to touch a milk float for perfect transport,
and I was sorry when the trip ended at my gate and I had to
wave goodbye to Mr Stanley.

The business of lifts to and from school I soon had organized.
It began, I think, with an offer from Mr Curtis of Julian
Brimstone Farm, one wet lunch time. He had been to the
Post Office in his van, saw me emerging from school, and
kindly ran me home through the puddles. This was such a
superior alternative to the mile-and-a-quarter footslog home
and back that I began to take note of regular transport which
ran at times convenient to my school hours.

On Wednesdays, I was sometimes lucky enough to catch
Mr Tutt's van. He was a fishmonger, and we dealt with him
regularly. Occasionally, Mr Groom the baker went our way.
Mr Smallwood, the other baker, drove a smart gig on his
rounds, but would not be prevailed upon to give lifts. I was

sorry about this, as he had a particularly handsome pony, and I should have relished a ride behind it.

But my most enjoyable lift was on Monday afternoons when the corn chandler Hodsall drove a massive cart, heavy with sacks of grain, seeds, cattle food and the like through the village just as we came out of school.

He was a slow taciturn man. Now I come to think of it, he was probably not Mr Hodsall himself, but I always thought of him so. I don't suppose we exchanged more than a dozen words during our journey. He sat, the reins slack across the great back of his cart horse, with a clay pipe upside down in his mouth.

I was content to watch the swaying back, surrounded by the wholesome smell of grain, and leaning against one of the sturdy sacks, my legs dangling from the wooden plank that served as a bench.

He pulled up outside my house without a word, getting down himself to grope under the wagon for the skidpan which hung from a chain beneath it. He took no notice of my thanks, affixed the skidpan as advised by the wooden notice on the bank, clambered up again, and set off, wordless, down the hill.

I was never a pony-mad little girl, but I loved these horses which I met now and again, and was glad that I experienced, for a short time, that fast-dying era of horse-drawn transport. Later, I was to make use of some of these memories when I began to write novels.

Accepting, or asking for, lifts from strangers was taboo, of course, and my parents made this plain, but they knew my benefactors well by this time and, knowing the pleasure I derived from my rides, they appreciated the kindness which prompted them.

BEGINNING TO QUESTION

WHEN I was promoted from Miss Ellis's class to the other side of the marmalade-coloured partition I sat in a desk with Norah and was under Mr Clarke's tutelage.

At least, for most of the day I was under Mr Clarke's eye, but when our daily Arithmetic lesson occurred, I was banished to my former standard as I was so backward in the subject.

I had managed to struggle along with the four rules in hundreds, tens and units, and even in pounds, shillings and pence, thanks to my early grounding, but when awful problems about Arthur having twice as much pocket money as Gwendolin, although only a third of Ned's, I began to falter. As for dripping taps over baths, express trains passing each other, and all the rest of standard five's problems, they were far too much for me, and it was from then on that I was the despair of innumerable mathematics teachers until I was eighteen. After that, no one bothered, much to my relief.

But the rest of the day was spent in the happy company of Norah and the top classes of the school. Mr Clarke was a cheerful man and we learned quite a lot, and Norah and I were delighted to be sharing a desk.

One day, Mr Clarke boomed at us:

> Norah and Dora
> Don't talk
> Any more-a.

which we considered the height of wit. I hope we stopped
exasperating him, at least for a time, but we had so much to
talk about that I am sure the chatter continued.

The school day was pretty regular. It began with prayers,
then a Scripture lesson, ghastly Arithmetic, playtime, then
Geography or History. Somewhere, fitted in, was a lesson
called Drill, which took place in the playground and consisted
of exercises done in four lines or teams. For this, the boys
took off their jackets, and we girls stuffed our skirts into our
knickers. No one changed footwear so that boys with iron
studs in their boots skidded about rather alarmingly.

We also played ring games such as 'Twos and Threes', and
sometimes rounders.

In the afternoon, on Mondays, Wednesdays and Fridays, we girls returned to Miss Ellis's care and faced Needlework. I was about as competent at this as at Arithmetic, and was usually allowed to practise different sorts of hems on a piece of unbleached calico which smelt of dog biscuits and was soon spotted with blood-pricks. Occasionally, I was given the lowly task of polishing the steel knitting needles with a limp scrap of emery paper, while my clever contemporaries tackled aprons, and handkerchief sachets, and kettleholders. As far as I was concerned, rubbing away with my emery cloth, they were welcome.

Meanwhile, the boys were busy with something called Mechanical Drawing which involved a lot of work with rulers and pencils, copying cones and other large geometrical shapes set before them on Mr Clarke's desk. I suppose it trained their eyes and hands for some sort of future work, but it cannot have been much fun.

Once a week, we had a much freer and easier drawing and painting lesson altogether, and we were supposed to bring something to the class for our subject. The girls were usually fairly responsible and arrived bearing a rose or daffodil, or perhaps a toy or an ornament from home, on which to try their skill.

The boys invariably had forgotten to bring anything, and, as the afternoon school bell tolled, there was a mad rush to a privet bush in a nearby garden. The irate householder invariably emerged to protest at this wholesale assault on his hedge, but by that time the boys were halfway up the school steps.

After playtime in the afternoon, things grew suitably easy, and we recited, or sang from *The National Song Book* or had a story read to us or, better still, enjoyed something billed as Silent Reading when we could get on with our own books.

It was a well-ordered life, if a trifle slow, and we were content.

Sometimes the day was enlivened by a visit from someone from the outside world. Mr Fox, one of the managers, occasionally called to see if we were all present and correct, and read our names aloud from the register. We responded with 'Here, sir.'

My name, as always, caused difficulty, and Mr Fox delighted our class by pronouncing it as 'Sharfer' on one occasion, and 'Shaffey' on another. It took some time for me to live this down.

Another manager was Mrs Richford, a kind and motherly lady who was more than welcome as she always brought a large tin of fruit drops with her. We all loved a visit from Mrs Richford.

Now and again, we had a visitor from other and more distant parts. One that I remember came to give us a lecture on the evils of DRINK, although at our age we had not met with much temptation in that line.

However, he gave us a fiery address, and hung a collection of diagrams over the blackboard which showed the result of consuming alcohol on various organs of the body. These were in colour, a horrid tangle of incomprehensible tubes, and when the picture of a drunkard's heart was displayed, one of the big boys slipped quietly under his desk in a dead faint and had to be carried into the fresh air amidst general sympathy.

I was particularly sorry as he had recently asked me to be his sweetheart, which I took to be a step towards matrimony. However, fond of him as I was, I now felt that I could not face a future with one quite so frail, and felt obliged to decline the honour, some days later, when he had completely recovered. He bore the reverse so well that I suspect that he had probably forgotten all about the offer.

I had a number of proposals about this time which, to be

honest, I found rather a nuisance, especially as they seemed to come from boys I had hardly noticed before. One proposal came when I was particularly busy fishing for frogs' spawn in our pond. You know how it is when you are collecting frogs' spawn, such heavy, awkward, slippery stuff, particularly if equipped with only a wobbly butterfly net and a one-pound jam jar, and I really could not give my full attention to his plea. In any case, I told him, as I struggled with my task, I really preferred Alan, and if he asked me then I should accept him.

My suitor said that he quite understood, but if I changed my mind, or Alan did not come up to scratch (and he didn't), then his offer still stood.

I can't help thinking that he must have grown up into a very nice man.

As quite a number of children came from a distance and could not get home to lunch and back, as I did, they brought a meal with them, for organized school dinners were many years ahead.

Once or twice, in very hot weather, I remember that I took sandwiches which my mother had prepared. They were wrapped in greaseproof paper and packed in a Palm Toffee tin, and there was usually an apple for dessert.

We were allowed on fine days to take our meal to the village recreation ground, some hundred yards away, and there to picnic, and it was on one of these occasions that I felt some shock in seeing one or two of my fellow picnickers' repasts. Two thick slices of white bread and a cube of cheese seemed to be their lot, but what really staggered me was the fact that the food was wrapped in newspaper. There were even greyish smears on the bread from the newsprint, but all was demolished with gusto, to my secret bewilderment.

More shocks awaited me. One little girl asked me to go with her to the shop, and there she asked for 'a specked orange', which mystified me. The crate was obligingly sorted over, and an orange handed down by the shopkeeper, and the child gave a halfpenny for it.

'What is a specked orange?' I asked on our way back to school. She showed me a dark brown spot on its peel.

'But it's going bad!' I protested.

'That's why it's cheap,' she told me. 'It's specked.'

This exchange appalled me. Heaven knows we were far from rich ourselves, but my mother, who was an excellent cook, would never have allowed us to eat doubtful food, let alone set out to buy it.

This incident gave me a great deal to think about. There were obviously different standards, and the one I had grown up to accept, and never questioned until now, might not be the correct one after all. My schoolfellow had enjoyed that specked orange. She had eaten it hungrily, and even nibbled the marred skin with relish. Furthermore, she had been pleased to have bought something cheaply. The whole transaction had given her satisfaction. Could it be that my mother was over-careful? Was a specked orange good value for a half-penny? Was it right to reject it, as I would have done, and to have paid twice as much for a perfect orange? It was a puzzle.

Perhaps grown-ups were not always right after all.

PERILS AND PASTIMES

THE happy months slipped by, and every one brought fresh discoveries, and I probably learnt as much on my walks to school as I did in the classroom.

Spring brought not only violets and primroses, but fleshy toothwort which I found under a cluster of elm trees. The honeysuckle put forth some of the first new leaves, and the walnut trees at Julian Brimstone Farm were auburn with young foliage.

In the summer, I discovered silverweed, its feathery foliage flat in the chalky dust at the side of the road, and its bright yellow flowers, like shallow cups, which smelt of almonds. The crab apple tree dropped small unripe fruit, no bigger than marbles, covered in grey velvet.

In the autumn came the joy of hazel nuts and walnuts and a plenteous supply of blackberries in the hedges.

And in the winter, despite the intense cold of those wind-swept North Downs, there was still plenty to admire. Snow could drift into piles which hid the hedges, swirling into fantastic shapes like clouds. Holly berries and yew berries lit their dark foliage, and gave promise of Christmas.

There were hazards as well as joys on my journeys. For one thing, the geese at Julian Brimstone Farm sometimes emerged from the yard, and wandered about in the road, picking up grit or pecking at the grassy verge by the flint wall.

They strongly resented anyone passing through their territory and set up a terrible honking cacophony as I attempted to edge past them. No wonder the Romans kept them as watch dogs!

Worse still, they would pursue me, hissing malevolently, snake-like necks outstretched, eyes as cold and blue as the aquamarines in my mother's pendant. With wings flapping, they could get up a fine turn of speed and, fleeing from them one day, I fell in the gritty road and barked both knees.

My lamentations brought forth Mr and Mrs Curtis, and I was taken into the farm kitchen and given first aid. The gentle swabbing I understood, but when Mr Curtis dipped a wing feather, probably dropped by one of my adversaries, into a bottle of iodine, and stroked the fiery stuff over my wounds, it was as much as I could do to quell my shrieks and to try to appear suitably grateful.

In the summer there was another problem. Wasps liked to make their nests in the banks bordering the lane, and normally we could give them a wide berth and hurry by safely. But one day, a naughty boy who was with us, thrust a stick into the hole and stirred up the contents.

Rightfully incensed at this treatment, the wasps fizzed out of the hole and attacked us. I was wearing my mackintosh, and two or three of the monsters got inside and stung me fiercely.

I was as furious as the wasps, and we all set about the boy who had disturbed them. As far as I can remember, he had no stings at all, as you might expect in this unjust world.

But except for such mishaps as these, we were a remarkably healthy lot, and I can't remember the First Aid box at school ever being in much use.

People had far fewer potions and pills in their homes then. Our own medicine box housed only such simple things as tins of Vaseline, boracic ointment and boracic powder which was dissolved in warm water to cure eye troubles.

A large roll of pink lint for spreading on grazed knees and a few rolls of bandages in different widths, with a bottle of medical disinfectant, took up most of the room. The narrowest bandage was used to make 'dollies' on battered fingers.

A large brown jar of mixed cod liver oil and malt was a fixture in the cupboard during the winter months, and a revolting white mixture called Scotts' Emulsion stood hard by, with a picture of a fisherman with an enormous fish draped over his shoulder and down his back, on the label. These aids to health were largely for the benefit of my sister, who suffered from coughs in the winter, but I was obliged to gulp down some of the stuff now and again. Other winter ills, such as chilblains and chapped faces, were treated with Melrose for the former, and Pond's Cold Cream for the latter.

In the summer, stings were usually dabbed with a Reckitt's blue bag, and sunburn eased with calamine lotion or witch hazel.

But, on the whole, our family and my school friends thrived in the boisterous downland air. Certainly those winters were enough to toughen up anyone, and of necessity we had plenty of exercise.

Other activities cropped up. As well as my music lessons, I was enrolled as a Brownie, and meetings took place once a week.

Our Brown Owl was a daughter of one of the big houses in the village, so that we had the run of large and well-kept grounds for learning such things as woodcraft, lighting camp fires, and recognizing a variety of plants and trees.

There was a summer-house available for wet days, and here we struggled with knots, granny, reef, clove-hitch, slip and a score more whose names I forget, and whose making I never completely mastered.

I liked my uniform and the tie pinned with a brass brooch with an elf on it, to show that I was in the elf patrol. I liked playing in the grounds of the noble Queen Anne house, but I was not really an ardent Brownie and never craved a sleeveful of badges as some of my friends did, and I actively disliked squatting in a ring and making hideous noises at the beginning and end of the session.

My sister was enrolled as a Girl Guide, but as her school activities were so arduous, she soon made her escape and was, I suspect, much relieved. We were never to become great joiners of societies and clubs.

We both played tennis on the new court, still remarkably uneven and needing to be marked out with a paint brush and a bucket of whitening. Neither of us was much good, but we helped to make up a four now and again when grown-up friends came to play with my father. I was allowed to serve from the halfway line, with my eight-and-a-half ounce racket.

My sister seemed to have a great deal of homework to do, and I felt sorry for her sitting with her books spread out on the dining table and working by the light of an Aladdin lamp.

She was a conscientious child and worried if things went wrong. She told me about life at her school, and bells which rang when a lesson ended, the trek to the rooms where some specific subject was taught, such as the Art room, the Chemistry laboratory, the Geography room, the Botany room, and so on.

There was something called 'the silence rule' which forbade talking on stairs and corridors. It would never do for Norah and me, I decided. There were desk inspections, and uniform inspections, and fortnightly reviews of work completed. Marks went from A to E, instead of something out of ten as in the village school. If you had three Es in a row, it seemed that you were sent to detention – a terrible disgrace. On top of that, she had the train journey which involved changing at Orpington station, and invariably meant a wait of anything up to half an hour.

It all sounded rather daunting to me, and ominously reminiscent of the great school which I had first attended – all bustle and endeavour, and trying to do better than the next child. My village school seemed much more delightful in comparison.

My parents, I knew, had high hopes of my joining Lil when I was eleven years old. A few children at my school sat for a scholarship examination early in the year, and Margaret from the Post Office was successful, and went on to Bromley where she did very well.

My Aunt Rose did her best to encourage my educational progress by keeping me supplied with such books as *Lamb's Tales From Shakespeare*, and *Golden Legends*, which contained stories from all over the world, and one particularly affecting one called 'The Children of Lir'. It was a horribly sad Irish tale about a princess who knitted vests from nettles for her brothers. I think they had been turned into swans, and this was the only way to turn them back into men. Looking back through the mists of time, I now wonder how she managed to transform nettles into knitting yarn. I found the whole thing deeply disturbing.

My parents too made valiant efforts to educate us, and we took a monthly magazine, edited by Arthur Mee, called *My Magazine*, and at the end of each year, the twelve issues were bound into one imposing volume.

It must have been somewhat exasperating for our parents to see that the first thing we turned to was a page of drawings and captions recounting the adventures of the Hippo Boys who were almost as enchanting as Mrs Bruin and her pupils in *Tiger Tim's Weekly* whose escapades I followed with rapture. However, quite a lot of general knowledge seemed to be absorbed from the more educational pages of *My Magazine* over the years, so that our parents' expenditure may have been justified after all.

When Lil was not heavily engaged in her school affairs, we still gave our dolls some attention, read voraciously, ran errands, helped our father in the garden, and our mother in the kitchen.

Occasionally we made toffee. It cost sixpence to make a meat tin full, and we bought the main ingredients at our nearest shop which was at the foot of the hill.

This village rejoiced, and still does of course, in the name of Pratts Bottom. The shop was kept then by an imposing lady called Mrs Bird.

We bought from her one pound of demerara sugar and a quarter of a pound of desiccated coconut. These two purchases took all our sixpence – the equivalent of today's two and a half pence.

Having trudged back up the hill, we put half a cup of water into a saucepan, a large lump of butter and let it melt.

Then we added the sugar and coconut and stirred assiduously. When it thickened, we turned the lovely mess into a meat tin, and tried to possess our souls in patience. Scraping the saucepan, and rasping the goo from the wooden spoon with our teeth, helped to pass the time.

Apart from the bliss of having such an enormous amount of sweet stuff all at once, there was the exquisite suspense of waiting to see if it turned out as *fudge* or *toffee*.

Either way, we were happy, and there were no prouder cooks in the kingdom.

WORK AND PLAY

THE Women's Institute had a considerable influence on our lives in those early days at Chelsfield.

The movement had been launched nationally not many years before, and my mother joined the local branch soon after we arrived in the village in 1921.

I suspect that my father encouraged her in this. Not only was she still recovering from major surgery, and cheerful company was good for her, but used as she was to London and its ways, I think my father may have thought that she might be lonely.

Even after their marriage, she had been in close touch with her mother, sisters and brothers, and immediately before the move to Chelsfield, she had been in daily contact with the family household at 267 Hither Green Lane.

My father was away from home from early morning until the evening, at his work in an insurance office in north London. It must have been a beast of a journey, probably involving three hours, at least, of the day in tedious travelling, but I never heard him complain.

It did mean, though, that my mother was alone except for my half-hour with her at lunch time, and no doubt my father was anxious for her to make friends.

The W.I. was exactly the right place to do this and had, in fact, been founded, as everyone knows, with this as one of its main aims.

My mother took to it like a duck to water, and very soon found herself secretary, which will come as no surprise to newcomers to villages everywhere.

Besides these clerical responsibilities with which she dealt competently, she was very keen on the other activities offered, and I well remember helping her to manhandle a dreadfully awkward and heavy pouffe to the Reading Room where upholstery classes were being held.

Cookery demonstrations particularly appealed to her, and we were willing guinea-pigs when she tried out new recipes on the family. Two which I recall were Cheese Aigrettes, a sort of savoury pancake, and Portuguese Soup which had a good amount of rice and tomatoes in it, and was as sustaining as it was delicious.

Friends were soon made, some of them the mothers of my own school fellows, including Norah's mother. If my father had entertained any fears about loneliness, they must have been quickly dispelled. The change from life in London suited her.

Something of its difference was brought home to me one afternoon when Aunt Rose was visiting us, and she and my mother were talking as they reclined in deck chairs. I lay on the grass, ostensibly reading, but ears cocked to hear the conversation.

It turned on my prospects of success in the future scholarship examination. Aunt Rose took an avid interest in our school progress, and sometimes passed on a message from our last revered headmistress Miss Pope, who had taken great pride in Lil's achievements and had hoped fondly that I would emulate her.

'You see,' Aunt Rose went on to say, 'she may be *happy* enough at this school, but does she get the same *stimulation*? I mean, town life has so much more to offer. More people, more points of view, competition with other children.'

I could have told her that absence of these three things was exactly what I liked best about my new school. I remembered the throngs of people in shops, dodging others on crowded pavements, enduring the racket in a town playground.

As for the stimulation of a town scene, it ranked as way down the list compared with the joys and excitement of a country lane, or our beloved oak and hazel wood. There was much which I had actively hated in the London streets I knew, as well as the noise. I was frightened of trains thundering over bridges above my head. I was afraid of the street hawkers, rag and bone men, cats' meat men, coal men, knife-grinders, all, in fact, who bellowed their services or wares with such ferocity.

The only good point about town streets was the hoardings with their advertisements, for upon these I could practise my newly-acquired skill of reading. My favourite was one advertising Nestlé's milk, and it showed two cats, one grey striped and skinny, the other round and white. Behind them was a night sky, complete with a moon, and below them was the verse:

> The ghost of Tabby
> Fed on skim
> Is all the war
> Has left of him.
> But Nestlé's is
> Full cream to the brim.

Attractive as I found this poster, chiefly because I adored cats, it could not make up for the many horrors of travelling about London. If this was what Aunt Rose termed 'stimulation', I could do without it.

Besides, I *did* see people. There were my friends at school, the grown-ups such as Miss Hill, Mr Curtis, Mr Hodsall and Mr Stanley who were kind to me, and whose company I enjoyed. And as for aunts, uncles and cousins, they were frequent visitors and provided a certain amount of gentle competition when we played pat-ball tennis or French cricket.

Furthermore, these encounters came in small numbers, often a one-to-one confrontation, with plenty of time to spare, and peace in which to savour the relationship. I had seen hordes of children in my old school playground, and knew hardly any of them. At Chelsfield, I knew and appreciated them all.

I hope that my mother did not take her older sister's words too much to heart. (One should always take sisters' advice with a pinch of salt.) But she was ambitious for her two daughters and, as I have mentioned earlier, I think she may have wondered if my new school would give me as good an education as the old one.

She need not have worried. I may have had to go down two or three standards in Arithmetic lesson, but my knowledge of flowers, trees, birds and animals had burgeoned, and my affection for my new friends grew as steadily as my physical well-being which flourished in this blissful country setting.

Apart from Arithmetic, I found the work at school not too arduous. Mr Clarke was not a hard taskmaster. His lessons were interesting and he encouraged questions.

He was of an equable disposition, and I can never remember him in a rage. He had made a comfortable niche for himself in the village and lived in the school house next door. He took part in village affairs, and aired his beautiful bass voice in the church choir.

He had a pretty wife, whom we schoolchildren only saw rarely, when she was hanging out washing or doing some other job in the garden which ran along beside the boys' playground.

Their two little boys we often saw playing there, or about in the village with their mother. Sometimes they ventured into the playground when the gate in the fence between our property and theirs had been ajar. I can remember our delight when two young faces appeared at the window high above, and behind, Mr Clarke's desk.

Alerted by our mirth and inattention, he soon summed up the situation and dashed out to rescue the intruders. It was as well that he did, for they had climbed upon two or three

ancient and rickety desks, lodged against the outside wall, and anyone heavier than his two toddler sons could have capsized them.

At that time, quite a lot of written work was done in our exercise books, and general neatness in handwriting was stressed far more than it is these days. Although I never mastered the copperplate writing which my fellows used, I got along pretty swiftly with my script, which now began to join up in a ham-fisted fashion rather like the Marion Richardson style which became fashionable some ten years later.

One afternoon a week, we had Composition lesson, a session heartily disliked by most of the pupils, particularly the boys. I must admit that the subjects set were somewhat pedestrian. 'A Day At The Sea', 'Helping Mother', 'A Trip To London' were typical of them. 'Helping Mother' no doubt was meant for us females to tackle. 'A Trip To London' probably did not get many takers for although we were only some seventeen miles from the capital, and could see the Crystal Palace winking in the sunshine against the smoky background of the city, there were still a number of children at Chelsfield who had never been to London or, for that matter, on a train to anywhere.

I quite enjoyed writing essays, and had no difficulty in spelling, probably because I came early to reading. But the boys made heavy weather of literary composition, and were forever breaking the silence by asking how to spell 'yesterday' or 'strawberries' or 'carpenter', the sort of words which, I felt impatiently, they could easily have worked out for themselves phonetically.

Mr Clarke used to take our efforts home, and return our books the next day, suitably marked in red ink. Occasionally, he read aloud from one of them, and if it happened to be mine, I was acutely embarrassed. I still think that it is a terrible ordeal to hear or see one's own work in public. Mr

Clarke's kind comments on my skill made me cringe. Much easier to bear were the subsequent teasings from the boys about my prowess.

This teasing was kindly. It had nearly killed them to write half a page on the subject set. That one younger than themselves could scribble two or three pages, struck them as peculiar to the point of being idiotic, and they were suitably indulgent.

As time went on, my initial alarm at having to share a classroom with boys gradually faded, and although my closest friends were girls, I began to look more tolerantly at the opposite sex.

I admired their physical strength. They were far better at digging, at trimming hedges, at lifting heavy things and particularly at climbing than we were.

The massive elm trees, which lined the road near St Martin's church, housed a noisy colony of rooks, and I watched one of the boys climb to the top of one of the trees to collect a

rook's egg. It makes me shudder now to remember the incident.

He descended neatly, the egg in his mouth for safety, and seemed absolutely unmoved by his feat. My own pride in being able to climb our small and accommodating yew tree paled into nothing beside this nonchalant exhibition.

On the whole, they were a hardy and agile set and would have been more agile still, I suspect, but for their tight clothing. Most of them wore thick jackets, some too tight and restricting, and the usual thick leather laced-up boots, often with iron-studded soles, meant that they were handicapped when it came to running and jumping.

We fared better as girls, in lighter clothing and sandals in the summer, although laced-up boots were certainly worn by some in the winter. Wellingtons, for general winter wear, did not come until later.

Our diet, by today's standards, would be considered too starchy, and viewing the contents of those lunches carried by my schoolfellows, this was certainly the case. I was lucky to go home to a well-cooked midday meal.

As well as the ubiquitous eggs at home, we now had plenty of goats' milk, for four goats had been added to the chickens, ducks, and rabbits already kept.

There was no shortage of fruit in the village generally, for beside the usual seasonal garden fruit, starting with rhubarb and gooseberries, and continuing throughout the summer months to the last late plums, the fields yielded splendid strawberries, and after the lorries had carted most of the crop up to Convent Garden, the farmers allowed the villagers to glean what was left.

We probably ate more than we collected for jam-making, but there were always plenty of jewel-bright jars put aside for the winter, and to be given to our poor town-bound relations when they visited.

On one or two occasions I was lucky enough to have my lunch at Groom's the baker's. My mother made the arrangement. For some reason she would not be at home, and I was excited at the thought of sitting in solitary state at one of Groom's marble-topped tables in front of the counter.

No one else ever seemed to have a meal there, although I believe cyclists sometimes came into refresh themselves with tea and buns in the afternoon.

My lunch cost sixpence, and was always the same. I had a boiled egg, bread and butter, and a glass of milk. After that I could choose one of Groom's three cakes, a currant bun, a doughnut or a fairy cake in a frilled paper case. Plenty of starch there, but no doubt I had an apple from home as well. I could hear sounds from the room beyond the shop, and sometimes a shadow was thrown on to the lace curtain which screened the glass door from prying eyes. Probably the eyes on that side were looking to see how I was getting on.

There was a large poster for Mazawattee tea which intrigued me. It showed an Edwardian lady in a velvet coat to the ground and an enormous hat, reclining on a green seat, like those I remembered in London parks.

She was dangling a little box from a gloved hand. Naturally it contained Mazawattee tea, and it was interesting to note that she had no other shopping. Why had she bothered to go to the shops just for that one item? And why had she collapsed on to the bench when even a lady as high-born as she obviously was, could reasonably have been expected to carry such a tiny parcel without undue strain? Or could she be taking it as a present to a distant friend, and was having a rest half-way? Perhaps she had suddenly decided that she could not part with such a treasure after all, and was sitting there before returning home with her parcel? I should like to have enquired of the girl who brought my lunch, and who took my sixpence once I had untied it from the corner of my handkerchief, but I was too shy.

I remembered, however, to thank her politely for looking after me, for my mother had pointed out that Groom's did not usually serve lunches, and we were much obliged to Mr Groom for making an exception in my case.

I suppose that lovely lady with her packet of tea ended on a bonfire one day.

What a pity!

PAGEANTS AND PEOPLE

O NE of those summers in the early twenties brought a memorable occasion.

The West Kent Women's Institute proposed to stage a mammoth pageant showing the history of the area, and it was to take place in the magnificent setting of Lullingstone Castle, only a few miles from the village.

The project was well thought out. At this distance of time, I could not say exactly how many scenes were envisaged, but something between a dozen or twenty would be my guess.

The first scene was to be about the coming of the Romans, and subsequent scenes showed local incidents in mediaeval times, a visit by Queen Elizabeth, a Civil War episode, some Georgian scenes and so on, up to the 1920s. The idea was to allot a scene either to one specific institute or several who were uniting to act one particular incident. The scenes were to be allotted by drawing names from a hat, so to speak, so that one had to abide by the luck of the draw.

Naturally, when this marvellous event was first mooted, all the ladies hoped for a scene in which they could dress in silks and satins, lace and ribbons, and wear magnificent wigs. The Stuarts were probably first choice – all those long curly wigs and dashing hats with ostrich feathers on the brim – but one or two still had a Victorian dress handed down from a forbear and it was agreed that little shawls, and even bustles, could be quite fetching.

Imagine the dismay at Chelsfield Women's Institute when it was discovered that they had been picked for Scene One, The Coming of the Romans. All thoughts of ostrich feathers, ringlets, or even plaits with pearls interwoven and wimples, had to be abandoned. Luckier institutes would swan about in this splendour, while the Chelsfield contingent would have to be content with clean sacks and old furs hacked into some rough semblence of Ancient Britons' clothing.

Unless, of course, they were Romans. The best-looking would undoubtedly be selected to form a Roman cohort, attired in gold-painted cardboard uniform and sandals, and whoever in charge at Chelsfield had to decide who should be an Ancient Briton and who should be an elegant Roman soldier, had a pretty sticky bit of diplomacy before them.

After the first disappointment, the local ladies set to with a will, sharing bits of old fur coats, getting excited about lengths of sacking, if they were Ancient Britons, and studying diagrams of Roman military costume – cardboard, gold paint and shears at the ready – if they were comely enough to have been chosen for the Roman cohort.

Children were needed, of course, as part of the tribe, and Norah and I were delighted to be dressed in the regulation sacks and furs, and to take part with our mothers.

Rehearsals were held in the garden of a lovely old house not far from the school, called Lilleys. I believe it was burnt down some years later. There, on hot afternoons, our mothers and other Britons limped about barefoot, dodging the pebbles on the gravel, and trying to look suitably engrossed in stirring imaginary pots, skinning imaginary rabbits, rocking imaginary babies, and occasionally rebuking their all-too-real excited children.

We loved it all, and when the great day arrived we piled into lorries supplied by Norah's father and made our way over the hill to Lullingstone Park, laden with various stuffed animals, an awkward pole with SPQR waving at the top for the Romans, pots, pans, large dolls for British babies and, of course, our picnic lunches.

We all agreed that it was a good thing to be on first, for after that we could sit back and enjoy the show. I remember how united we all felt, a real band of sisters, out to do our best, and to show the rest of West Kent that Chelsfield was a force to be reckoned with.

To be honest, I really don't remember much about the rest of the performance except that the splendid figure of Queen Elizabeth, played by Lady Hart-Dyke, if I remember rightly, on a fine grey horse, against the setting of Lulling- stone Castle and acres of Kent- ish greenery, has remained with me to this day.

I remembered this pageant when I wrote *Village Diary* years later. Mrs Pringle was then cast as an influential Ancient Briton, but I don't imagine that she enjoyed herself as rapturously as we did over sixty years ago.

The feeling of being part of a community, which had been so strong during the preparations for the pageant, was something which those born in the village naturally took for granted. As newcomers from London, it struck us all as something rare and valuable.

People's talents were known and respected. If a concert or fête were being organized then those in charge knew exactly where to look for support.

The former headmaster's daughter could be counted on for a display of dancing in the Isadora Duncan manner. Another girl was good at lettering and would undertake to do the posters. The Glee Club, to which my father and mother belonged, would render as required. Someone would be game to recite monologues, which would need to be carefully vetted if the rector was to be present.

The cake stall would groan under fruit cakes from Mrs This, shortbread from Mrs That, and Victoria sandwiches from my mother, who always had plenty of eggs.

What is more, these skills were employed willingly. Part of the fun of a village affair was the work that you put into it, and what each person could contribute was soon summed up.

My sister Lil, young as she was, was soon prevailed upon to play the church organ on the odd occasion when the usual organist was absent. I had a more lowly rôle as organ blower, when she was at the keyboard, and pumped a handle up and down in the vestry, one eye on a small weight which travelled between two pencil marks on the wooden screen. If it rose too high then the air ran out, and bedlam ensued. I learnt to dread Lil's pulling out of a stop marked TREMOLO, for then my little weight fairly galloped to the top mark in a series of bounds.

This knowledge of each other's talents extended to their clothes, their eccentricities, their homes and gardens. Neighbours were important, and could prove a blessing or a bane, according to temperament. As children, we frequently ran errands for nearby grown-ups.

On one occasion, our friend Peggy who shared our yew tree, was dispatched by an elderly neighbour of hers to the local ironmonger at Pratts Bottom. She was to order: 'An inexpensive enamel slop bowl', and it was to be delivered promptly.

This somewhat imperious old lady was the wife of a retired clergyman, and everything had to be done with the greatest rectitude.

We accompanied Peggy on her errand, wondering vaguely among ourselves exactly what 'an inexpensive enamel slop bowl' was, and what was its purpose.

Peggy thought it was for washing up. One of us hazarded a guess that it was some sort of basin for tea leaves, although why it should be made of *enamel* when presumably the rest of the tea set would be of *china*, we could not fathom.

'Well, I shall just repeat what she said,' said Peggy, 'and leave it to the shop man.'

We agreed that this was all that could be done, and duly delivered the message.

Luckily the proprietor seemed to know what was required, and we retired with relief to pursue our own pleasures.

Later, we heard that an enamel chamber pot, *not even swathed in paper*, had been left on the *front doorstep* of that respectable house, and poor Peggy and her mother endured the full force of their neighbour's indignation. Relations remained strained for some months, and Peggy went on strike and said she would never go shopping for anyone ever again.

She had our sympathy.

One of the most welcome errands I was called upon to undertake was the very occasional delivery of a telegram to a nearby neighbour.

Mrs Smith at the Post Office saw me one lunch time, and asked me to take the yellow envelope to our friends next door to my home.

I felt very proud to be entrusted with this official task, and even more overwhelmed when I was given *sixpence*, evidently

the statutory GPO fee, for my labours. Sixpence was a fortune then for a child, and no doubt it was rushed to Mrs Bird's for a pound of demerara sugar and a quarter of desiccated coconut.

Not many people received telegrams in those days, and far too few needed to be delivered by me, but what bliss when that occasion came my way!

The people I saw most of, naturally, were my school-fellows. As those three happy years slid by, I grew to view them with affection and admiration.

In many ways, they were older and wiser than I was. Most of the girls had younger brothers or sisters to look after, or seemed to do more for their parents than I was called upon to do. They were knowledgeable about such mysteries as the source of babies, in which I was not particularly interested as I had too many other enthralling things to do.

They noticed clothes, hair styles, and other people's possessions. The boys were not so much objects of attraction, as positive nuisances, demanding attention, being noisy, rough, and sometimes downright vulgar. The girls had a well-developed sense of propriety, and were often shocked at things which I sometimes thought merely amusing.

The school building became as familiar to me as my own home. I grew fond of the grooves in my desk lid, the knots on the floor boards, the reflection of the high windows in the dark background of the portraits of our King and Queen.

I liked the green metal contraptions high on the wall, which had a little metal fist, holding a short rod, on the outside. The boys used to lob their apple cores into them, and it was years later that I was told that these mysterious fixtures were ventilators. Heaven alone knows what sort of insanitary mess was inside!

I liked to hear the droning of the children next door, beyond the pitch-pine partition, as they chanted their tables or learnt a poem. I liked to feel the warmth from the coal fire, and to watch one of the big boys shovelling on the fuel when needed.

I appreciated Mr Clarke's witticisms, his tolerance, and his handling of the top standard boys who could have been obstreperous, so close were they to escape into a larger world.

In fact, the place fitted me as snugly as a cocoon, and lapped in warmth, security and friendship, I thrived as never before.

As the dreaded scholarship examination drew nearer, I began to realize just how keenly I should miss my present surroundings.

I had visited my sister's school in Bromley now and again, when there had been an Open Day or Sports Day, and of course had heard all about it from her.

It was here that a few of us from Chelsfield School sat the examination one Saturday morning in spring.

My heart sank at the sight of those long stony corridors, the vast hall, the plethora of classrooms, and the expanse of playing fields.

Everything was beautifully kept. The paintwork inside was glossy and white, a rare thing to find in a school. The parquet floors shine like satin. The glass in the doors and windows gleamed with cleanliness. There were neat flower beds set

among mown lawns, and I longed for something smaller, shabbier and familiar.

In the year before, Margaret from the Post Office had become a successful pupil here, and Mr Clarke had told us in assembly how proud we should all feel.

My heart had gone out to poor Margaret, compelled to stand alone before the school, enduring Mr Clarke's eulogy and – final horror – the clapping of her school-fellows. But she was an equable child, and bore it all very well.

The result of my own effort was not due until June, and I sensed that my parents were anxious. I hoped that I should not disappoint them, but I could hardly bear to think of leaving the village school.

On 17 June 1924, my parents received a letter to say that I had passed. The postman came about eight o'clock, and I was in the garden feeding my rabbits, before setting off for school.

I can see their faces now, full of loving pride, as they held up the letter and called the news to me.

My sandals were wet with dew, my fingers sticky with bran mash, but I hope that I raised a smile to match their own.

Two terrible clouds hovered over me. I should be going to a school just like my first one. It would be big, noisy and competitive. Examinations would loom larger every year. I should have endless possessions, three pairs of shoes, a satchel, a hateful uniform with a panama hat in summer and a black felt in winter. I should be bound round with rules, pestered by prefects, goaded by ambitious school mistresses, harried to death.

The second fear was more immediate. I should have to face the same horrors as Margaret. Would Mr Clarke take pity on me, and let me off the public praise? Could I get him not to let the children clap? Could I pretend to be ill and stay at home, preferably in the bathroom?

My mother wrote a note to Mr Clarke in case he had not yet heard the amazing news, and it was put into my pocket. She kissed me fondly as I set off. My father, wreathed in smiles, had already departed to Chelsfield station.

I made my way along the lane with my heavy burden. I walked past the violet beds, the walnut trees, the geese splashing in the pond, the shabby shed which housed the shabbier fire-fighting barrow, and came within sight of the school.

Vociferous and excited, my companions rushed about behind the railing, beneath the fluttering lime trees, their hair bobbing in the breeze.

I fingered the letter in my pocket, and mounted the school steps slowly.

A shadow had fallen across my sunlit world. It was never to be quite so bright and carefree again.

EPILOGUE

ONE winter morning, over half a century later, the telephone rang. One of the editors of a Sunday magazine asked if I would like to visit my old school and write an article describing it now, and when I attended it so many years ago.

Of course, Chelsfield School sprang to my mind as I listened to further details of length, payment, deadline and so on.

Luckily, I had the forethought to ask who else was contributing to this feature. A few eminent names floated down the wire, including Laurie Lee. My heart sank. Of course, he would write about his village school in Gloucestershire, and with all the skill and charm which I so admired.

'Tell me,' I said, 'Mr Lee is writing about his village school, I suppose?'

'Alas no! It's been closed. He proposes to write about a later school which he attended.'

It's an ill wind that blows nobody any good, and I replied buoyantly. 'In that case, I will visit my old village school in Kent, and let you have the result.'

★ ★ ★

I travelled down from Charing Cross by train, passing through the old familiar stations.

I did not go as far as Chelsfield Station, where I had first stood enraptured by early primroses and larks, for Norah met me at Orpington and drove me to her home at Well Hill.

She was now a grandmother, with lots of fluffy white hair, but her smile and her voice were as gentle as when we first met at the age of eight. Now her grandchild was at our village school, and I should see her there the next day on my official visit.

We woke to torrential rain, and were off in good time, following the school bus. When it stopped outside the school, Norah and I waited in the car watching the children mount those well-known steps to the playground above.

On a morning such as this, we should have arrived in our mackintoshes, shoes soaking, hair dripping, and generally bedraggled. Our successors stepped, dry and immaculate, from the shelter of the bus.

I followed them, half-dreading what I should find after fifty years. Surely, anything must be an anticlimax after the fond dreams I had nurtured for so long.

To my delight, the basic structure was the same, and the playground virtually unchanged, although a glass corridor ran along the back of the building where once Mr Clarke's small sons had climbed up on the desks to look into the classroom.

His house, too, had been incorporated into the school, and the sitting-room where he had lent me *David Copperfield* was transformed into the school kitchen. I felt uncomfortable there, as though I were a trespasser.

I spent the day with those children, and the kind and elegant young headmaster who showed me everything. It was still miraculously my old school – small, domesticated, secure, but wonderfully refined and beautified. Carpets covered the splintered floorboards whose shiny knots had reminded me of buttered brazil nuts. Bright pictures had taken the place of King George V and his wasp-waisted Queen, and the children themselves were clothed in garments which would have been unimaginably chic to us.

Two little girls discussed their ponies, and I remembered the awe with which my battered scooter had been greeted by my fellows in those distant days. School dinner was served, hot, fragrant plateful of well-cooked, properly balanced nourishment — although I noticed that greens were still left on the rims. A far cry indeed from those lumps of print-grimed bread I remembered.

There was so much to attract the eye, a tank of goldfish, shelves of bright books, enormous paintings being created with outsize brushes. I thought of the little boys who marched from Miss Ellis's class to Mr Clarke's, so long ago, rulers sticking out from their thick socks, as they made their way to a session of Mechanical Drawing. How much luckier their descendants were!

I spent a few minutes, towards the end of the day, alone in the wet playground. From inside, I could hear the hum of school activity. The lime trees were still there, dripping. The cold Kentish air struck the flesh as keenly as it had always done. The grey roof glistened, the iron railings were beaded with bright drops, a pigeon came down to strut through the puddles, and I was eight years old again.